Praise for *Neu*

New Story, New Power: A Woman's Guide to Negotiation is a welcome book for women needed in these changing times. Beth Fisher-Yoshida blends insights from the neurosciences (our mindsets) with stories (our narratives) to offer a practical guide for women as they negotiate in various parts of their lives.

—**Deborah M. Kolb, PhD**, author of *The Shadow Negotiation: How Women Can Master the Hidden Agendas That Determine Bargaining Success* and *Negotiating at Work: Turn Small Wins into Big Gains*

Fisher-Yoshida has effectively diagnosed what gets in the way of women confidently negotiating—our mindset and beliefs. Whether it's a work, family or relationship issue, addressing and reframing the stories we carry can help us experience successful negotiations.

—**Dr. Cindy R. Pace**, global chief diversity equity inclusion officer, MetLife; and lecturer, Columbia University

This is a book which transcends the traditional concept of negotiation and leads you on a personal and professional journey to understanding your best self and how to construct your own personal and highly effective narrative for all situations in your life. It guides the reader from understanding the origins of our own narratives and various professional and personal behaviors to the illuminating case studies of others and concludes with prescriptive lessons to carry with you as you venture forward each day. This book will be of great value to the young female professionals beginning their career journey and beyond to the seasoned female board director learning to navigate, influence, and achieve successful results in the boardroom!

—**Virginia Gambale**, chair of the board, Nutanix; technology leader; investor; and board director

This book provides a unique slant on both negotiation and women negotiators. Moving away from treating gender as individuals, it frames negotiation as relationships, ones grounded in contexts, narratives we hold, and situational circumstances. Each chapter begins with a different story that becomes reframed to show how women can change their narratives. Chapters focus on important negotiation contexts, such as workplaces, families, personal relationships, and deceptive situations. Adapting classic knowledge from the field, it provides tips on nuances in negotiation, managing emotions, dealing with power, and communicating effectively. I strongly endorse this book and consider it a MUST READ for all negotiation scholars and practitioners, including women.

—**Dr. Linda Putnam**, distinguished research professor and professor emerita, UCSB Communication Department

New Story, New Power

New Story, New Power

A Woman's Guide to Negotiation

Beth Fisher-Yoshida

BOLD STORY PRESS
Washington, DC

Bold Story Press, Washington, DC 20016
www.boldstorypress.com

First edition published January 2023

Library of Congress Control Number: 2022915752

ISBN: 978-1-954805-34-7 (paperback)
ISBN: 978-1-954805-35-4 (e-book)

Text and cover design by Laurie Entringer
Cover image: Lana Sham, Shutterstock
Illustrations by KP Designs
Author photo by Cole Giordano

Printed in the United States of America
10 9 8 7 6 5 4 3 2 1

To my mother,
who taught me the value
of loyalty and humor

Contents

Foreword

Like many of my business school classmates, I was very excited to take my first class in negotiations. It was one of the most popular courses, and I was ecstatic to get a spot. While many of my peers wanted to learn how to negotiate successfully to win, it was more complicated for me. The word "negotiations" raised both fear and curiosity. I had often dreaded negotiations, as they made me feel I had to fight aggressively in a winner-take-all situation. But I also wanted to learn real approaches that I could use to be more effective and less nervous. I greatly enjoyed the class and practiced a few times with classmates and on my family. However, I was still very early in my career and didn't yet know how critical these lessons would turn out to be down the road.

After spending more than 20 years in the financial services industry negotiating for new jobs, additional assignments, and increased compensation, I have personally seen the importance of negotiations to my career. Having seen other women across industries struggle to climb the corporate ladder, attain promotions, and get paid equally, I am convinced that negotiation skills are vital at all stages of women's professional lives. Whether it's breaking into new fields at the start of their careers, or staying in relevant and rewarding roles as they get older, women need these skills to thrive. They especially need them if they become working mothers and have to advocate for themselves while managing both work and family.

I have worked with thousands of professional women to help them advance both professionally and personally. In 2018, I launched Women on the Move at JPMorgan Chase.

It was the first full-time, global team dedicated to empowering women and girls inside and outside of the firm. Over the years, I have advised women small business owners and startup founders on growing and scaling their businesses, educated girls and women on personal finance topics, and coached women employees at all levels. Negotiations is a skill needed by all of them, in every setting, to achieve their goals.

When I set out to design a development program for mid-career women, I asked them what skills they needed help on the most. Across the board, the resounding answer was negotiations. Women knew they could use the training to go further. So, we implemented negotiations as a key component of our program, and it's always our most popular module. Women appreciate the idea that they can negotiate beyond compensation, such as for additional responsibility, stretch projects, more resources and training. They are inspired by the stories of others who have faced obstacles and negotiated to better meet their needs.

One thing that typically surprises women is that negotiations are a very gendered exercise. For starters, men tend to be more aggressive, ask for more, and achieve better results. Even if women are equally skilled at it, they can be labeled "too aggressive" and be penalized for being tough. Our societal norms have long influenced the perception of women as nurturing and more focused on community and family rather than themselves. This is a deep-rooted stereotype that is very difficult to change. Once women understand the full range of strategies they can use to overcome gender bias, they can flex their approaches to ensure their messages are better received.

Beth Fisher-Yoshida understands this on a deep level. I have known her since the start of my tenure running Women on the Move. In the first few months of my new role, she invited me to be a keynote speaker at WIN Summit. It's a powerful annual event that teaches negotiations to women.

It was my first time speaking publicly on women's issues, and I was grateful to hear Beth lay out the case for women to improve their skills.

I could see immediately why Beth was such a compelling teacher. She's studied and practiced negotiations for 30 years and knows what works. Through hundreds of interviews and workshops around the world, she has seen the issues women are wrestling with and how they can improve their skills in a way that feels authentic and neutralizes gender bias. I wish I had first learned negotiations under her, so that I could have learned earlier what to do differently.

As you'll see in this book, Beth has provided a master class in negotiations. She shares the powerful research behind why we think the way we do and how this influences our approach to negotiations. She also provides us with suggestions on how to break out of old habits and learn new ways of seeing and doing things. As you gain the skills needed to better prepare and conduct negotiations, you will feel more confident in your ability to achieve the outcomes you desire. The tools in this book are practical, and the case studies are extremely relatable—they address the challenges that are common to us all.

Negotiation is one of the most powerful tools to achieve professional and personal fulfillment. We use it every day, even if we do not realize it. By helping us get more out of life, negotiation plays a huge role in our success and our well-being. In reading this book, you have taken the first step towards mastering an important skill. Take the next step and practice often, so that you will be well prepared for bigger-stake negotiations. Please also share Beth's book with your friends, sisters, mothers, and other women in the work force, so that you, too, can help more women succeed.

Samantha R. Saperstein
Head of Women on the Move, JPMorgan Chase
December 2, 2022

Introduction: Women and Negotiation

The word *negotiation* can be a trigger for some women. The mention of it and the thought of bargaining for something important can be daunting. Having to engage, maybe with difficult people, can seem to be an insurmountable task, causing some women to shy away, freeze, or wilt during the negotiation; other women come in fired up to be tough, only to leave badgered and frustrated. Of course, many women do negotiate successfully, and there are probably numerous moments of success along the way, even if the final result is not completely what was wanted. If negotiating is not all bad news, why do women associate negative emotions with the thought and act of negotiating?

I began to wonder why there was so much emotion surrounding this word, especially for women. So, I began exploring. I read many books, interviewed many women, studied negotiation, taught, directed a masters' level program in negotiation, developed negotiation workshops, and revised negotiation strategies for organizations. I also became uber sensitive to what I and others around me were doing during negotiations. I now think I have a better understanding of what it takes for women to become effective negotiators. I do not have all the answers, but I do know that we can absolutely improve our negotiating abilities. To do so, we must want to change our stories about who we are as negotiators. This book is about the stories we tell ourselves and what we can do to change the stories and become more effective negotiators.

While changing one's story may not seem to lead to better skills as a negotiator, in fact doing so often generates results rather quickly. At times you may feel you are taking two steps forward and one step back, but the approach still produces a forward-moving trajectory. If you are on board to consider this change, you may be asking what story needs to be changed and where these stories come from in the first place.

Our stories come from many sources, including our family, teachers, community members, religious leaders, and the media (don't forget the pervasive role media plays in most aspects of our lives), including social media. Almost constant messaging comes to us, directly—and indirectly—about how we should be, what we should think and do, and how we should act. Many of these messages are gender-based, and some place women at a disadvantage in the realm of negotiation.

A male-dominated world has defined the act of negotiation as two (or more) parties facing each other and demanding their share.[1] This definition might be an exaggeration because the demands may be presented as requests and the negotiations may take place over multiple sessions, include relationship building, and have someone in the middle to smooth over the quality of the interaction.

Women can certainly learn how to perform under those conditions, but the style contradicts some of the stories women have learned about what it means to be a woman. This is part of the challenge women face. Research shows how women are conditioned to act when interacting with others, although these profiles have been challenged over the years.[2] Women are often characterized as nurturing and likeable. At the same time, women have been encouraged to take what they want because being nurturing and likeable may be fine, but it may not get them what they want. So, women are encouraged to be assertive. However, when women assert "too much," they are labeled with all sorts of terms that are not endearing.

How much is too much assertion? Here is an illustration of a woman asserting herself in the context of a negotiation:

> *Thank you for meeting with me, John. I see there is a more senior position available, and I am planning on applying for it. I have been working here for almost two years, have had successful project outcomes, and I have the qualifications for it. I am asking you for a recommendation to support my candidacy.*

On an assertiveness continuum with not enough on one end, too much on the opposite end, and just right in the middle, how would you rank the woman in this scenario?

There is no fixed amount of assertiveness we should display; the level of assertiveness depends on the situation, style, wording, timing, and all sorts of other variables that cannot be addressed with a formula. Men do not have these same issues because from an early age they are given the message that they can assert themselves to get what they want. Go back to the scenario described above and now picture that the person speaking is a man instead of a woman. How would you rank the man in that scenario? If you came up with different assessments, that says something about perception, perspective, and the story you tell yourself about assertiveness for a man and for a woman.

Several of the women I interviewed mentioned that when they went on job interviews early in their careers, they did not know they could even ask for a certain salary or benefits. They learned to ask much later on in their professional lives. Research shows that men do not face the same challenges.[3] This is not to say that men do not have challenges, but that is a different book on a different day. Currently, gender is viewed as a social construction (by some), and this raises the question of the purpose and value of gender traits and associations since, in some circles, gender fluidity is the norm.

Regardless of how you classify yourself according to gender, you can assume you are being gender-classified by your negotiating partner.[4] As such, the other person will assume certain characteristics about you and respond to you accordingly. For example, if women are supposed to be likeable, and you assert yourself more than the other person deems suitable, you may be labeled as aggressive and responded to according to that labeling. It will not go well. You will no doubt feel disappointed with the encounter, because if you have been successfully conditioned as a woman, you are seeking to be liked and approved of because women are supposed to be nice and not make waves.

If the vibes you are getting from the other party contradict that profile you have bought into all these years, you may end up not feeling good, and then negative thoughts like, "Now you've done it. You overstepped your boundaries," end up in your head in a recurring script like preprogrammed sheet music in an old-fashioned player piano. That inner dialogue cannot be helpful in a negotiation. It undermines effectiveness because *how you act in the negotiation is influenced by the story you tell yourself about who you are as a negotiator*.

Our stories of who we are are developed and influenced over the years by the world around us. These stories shape our belief systems, and these beliefs, even if not conscious, determine our actions.[5] If the messaging we received as women encouraged us not to make the first move because that might be received as too assertive, then our move is second, made in response to the other person's initial move. In negotiation, the first move is known as the anchor, and it sets the initial position in the negotiation. Going second places our opening move as a response to this anchor,[6] which may be very different from what we wanted our opening move to be.

Of course, we can always ignore the anchor and establish our own first move, which upsets the flow of the negotiation and can also have us engaging in parallel monologues and not actually negotiating. Negotiating requires interaction, and if each negotiator proceeds on his or her own path, the negotiation will fail.

Why This Book Now?

There are other negotiating books in the market—some really good ones—and there are books about what women should and should not do when they are in a negotiation.[7] But because there is no one single set of characteristics describing the varied roles women play in society, there are contradictory messages about what women should and should not do. There is research, for example, showing that white women, while earning less than white men, still earn more than women of color.

Payscale, founded in 2002, wanted to bring transparency to salary scales. They have been collecting data through online surveys across gender and industries. Their most recent research in 2021 showed that the median salary in uncontrolled settings—in other words, the median salary for all women regardless of type of work or level—is on average $0.82 for every $1.00 earned by white men. This is also known as the opportunity gap. Another way to frame this is that the research shows the median salary for men is about 18% higher than for women. When race enters the equation, the pay gap is even wider to be as low as some groups of women of color earning $0.69 to every $1.00 white men earn. Calculating this over the lifetime of a career can add up to hundreds of thousands of dollars.[8]

In addition, we have more than one persona, and when considering the interconnectedness of all the different facets of who we are, we add layers of complexity and nuance to building our character.[9] We have our gender orientation, our race, religion, professional classification, family designations; we are friends, colleagues, and so on with each of these roles creating its own persona. We move in and out of these roles, some with more fluidity than others.

The increase in the publication of books urging women to ask, be assertive, take more, puts the onus on us. If we do not ask, we will not receive, so regardless of our mindset, skill set, and contextual circumstances, the burden of deciding our own fate is totally on us. Well, yes and no. Adopting this new mindset can cause confusion between the messaging heard on a regular basis since childhood and the reality of what is actually happening now in the workplace and in our everyday lives. There are so many different types of influences that shape any given moment and interaction, that an established set of principles and practices will need to be adapted for the situation on a case-by-case basis. There is no one rule that fits all.

We also know more now than ever about the way our brains work[10]. We know that men's and women's brains are wired differently, and the actions of the genders create different patterns because of these initial wiring differences.[11] However, even this understanding has room for modification. There are some differences that are not uniform across genders. In addition, the nature versus nurture debate continues, as our social environments also influence our brains, their configurations, and how we compensate based on what we need to do in certain circumstances.

There are social and cultural norms that create different narratives by which we live, including the stories in our heads and the self-talk in which we engage.[12] Some of these stories are helpful, and some get in our way. We learn these stories from our families, schools, communities, and these social stories are all around us, some more explicit than others. Our moral compass is also learned from these sources and the values that are deeply embedded within us.

These stories are not separate from what takes place in our brains. Words have an impact on us in multiple ways, including making patterns in our brains.[13] These patterns make it more likely for us to repeat the responses to situations because they set the tracks in our brains. The "neurons that fire together wire together," aligning words we use with creating these brain tracks and influencing our behavior. It works so that what we hear shapes our brains, creates the stories we have about ourselves, and influences our behavior. Our behavior, in turn, influences the responses we get from others, influencing our brains and behavior and the stories we have about ourselves. It is a continuous cycle and feedback loop.

The Stories We Carry

It does not matter if we say our story aloud for others to hear or if we tell the story to ourselves. The point is that hearing the story has powerful effects on our brains and behavior.[14] Women are conditioned to believe that we are nurturers, with a set of behaviors that fits this framing. We want to do what good nurturers do because we want to be accepted, and the need to be accepted can mean more to us than asserting ourselves to obtain our own wants and desires that may be short-term anyway.[15]

There is risk and reward involved either way. If we seek what we want while trying not to upset the apple cart, we may receive less than we ultimately desire. Or we might take bigger leaps of faith and pursue what we want at the risk of not being liked and accepted. There is an upside and a downside to all our actions. The stories we heard that socialized us into the world may conflict with the personal stories of what we want, including our ambitions and aspirations. It is a useful practice to question why the rules and patterns of behavior we are expected to uphold were established in the first place and by whom. Who do they serve, and how are we served by perpetuating them? Ultimately, we need to make decisions about the choices we have instead of letting others make decisions for us.

We might be aware that the status quo is not providing what we want or allowing us to feel accomplished or achieve states of bliss. However, while we may have this awareness, we do not necessarily know what to do to change things. We also may not be up for the challenge because with any new set of ideas and behaviors comes the discomfort that accompanies the unknown.

We all have different levels of tolerance for ambiguity.[16] Those of us who are better able to tolerate ambiguity can allow an issue to remain unresolved for the moment.[17] Those of us who are less tolerant will seek to find answers to our unresolved questions, although we may be anxious in the process. It is good to consider which discomfort we are choosing: maintaining the unsatisfactory status quo or changing by exerting agency and trying to make a positive difference.

This book takes you through a process that will strengthen your negotiation skills by working on changing the narrative and self-talk in your head that governs the choices you make and helping you negotiate a better life.

What Is Happening Today?

At the time of this writing, we are transitioning out of a global pandemic, and many people are continuing to work remotely. This increase in virtual communication and interaction has had a number of effects on women and how they negotiate. Studies done during the pandemic reflect that fewer women asked for raises and workplace benefits than men.[18] In addition, unemployment rates for 2020 almost doubled from what they were in 2019.[19] Women have higher unemployment rates than men, and the pandemic exacerbated this phenomenon. Women were expected to take care of family and school their children who were at home during the pandemic. Payscale also noted that on average women receive 4% less on new job offers if they are unemployed at the time of getting a new job. Women are vulnerable to these types of changes in everyday life circumstances.

Creating Our Story and Asserting Agency

Advances in research on social construction of language,[20] emotions,[21] neuroscience, and neuroplasticity demonstrate that we have a lot more agency about how we want to be in the world. (A social constructionist view means that language and emotions, for example, are not necessarily universal or the same for everyone, but that we create them in our interactions with others.[22]) This shift away from a classical view of communication and emotions emphasizes that our communication patterns can be changed,[23] and this means that acquiring knowledge and skills enhances our abilities to make different and new patterns of connections and relationships through communication.

For example, instead of continuing to respond in the following manner, think of alternative responses:

> Jim and Alice take turns cooking and cleaning up afterwards. Alice tends to do more of the cooking, and when Jim cleans up, he washes the pots but not the lids. Alice does not understand this and she gets annoyed because then she ends up having to wash the lids. Her typical response is to ask Jim why he

did not wash the lids. Jim gets offended that she is questioning him and feels that she does not appreciate what he does. This pattern continues to repeat itself day after day, week after week.

If Alice wanted to change the pattern of their communication she could respond in several ways: She could ignore the unwashed lids and hope that Jim washes them on his own; She could thank him for washing the pots and not mention the lids, hoping he will feel appreciated and in turn wash the lids; She could do both the cooking and washing up herself; She could ask Jim to cook more often; and she would clean up after dinner. Whatever she chooses will disrupt the previous pattern and create a new one. Alice has choices about how she responds and the communication dynamics she creates.

One challenge that has been a deterrent for some is that with asserting agency and making these choices comes responsibility,[24] and that may not be desirable because then we can be held accountable when things do not work out according to our plan or desire. As daunting as this may seem, we need to recognize that we have choices and may have always had choices, even if they seem to place us between a rock and a hard place. This book prepares you to act on those choices in more constructive ways that benefit you and those around you.[25]

This also leads us to question the social construction of gender and to consider how these constructions create prototypes of what an ideal man or woman should be. We need to question how useful these constructions still are and whether they continue to serve us and in what ways they are helpful when it comes to negotiation strategies and tactics. In addition, the binary profiles of gender have been tested and challenged in different communities that support more gender fluidity and less distinctive boundaries between the genders.

Processes and Outcomes

Negotiation consists of processes and outcomes, which are interconnected.[26] In order to change the outcomes we must change the processes in which we engage (Figure 1). To change the processes, we must change the narrative, and therefore we must change our mindsets and attitudes about who we are as negotiators to enable us to change the story we have about ourselves and the inner dialogue that reflects those thoughts. Then we learn and practice new skills that continue to make this new story of who we are as negotiators a reality. We create new pathways in our brains and enact behaviors that continue to support these new pathways. As these pathways are used, they are reinforced, making it more likely that we will behave accordingly.

Imagine it, and it will be.[27] More advanced methods of research and the ability to see brain activity have shown that when we create a vision of our desired future, that vision has a good chance of coming to fruition. One part of this is to visualize the outcomes we want. To support the desired outcome becoming a reality, we then have to believe in it and develop the skills to make it happen so that it becomes a part of our behavior.

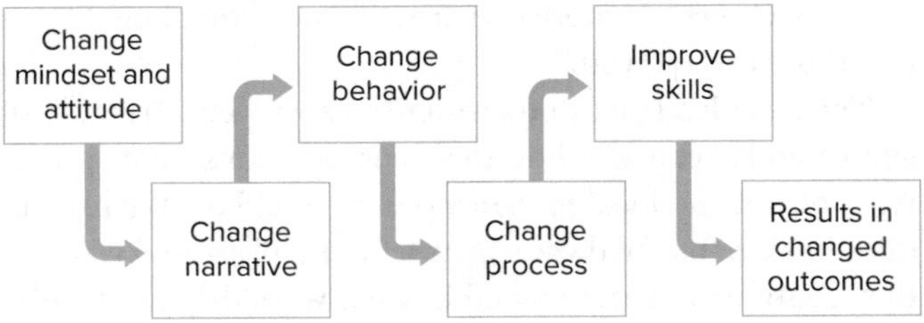

FIGURE 1 Process for Changing Outcomes

A change process that results in a different outcome requires shifts in mindsets, behaviors, and more, and they are all interconnected.

We can visualize speaking up at a meeting and then become more specific in our visioning to accomplish this goal. For example, we can prepare something in advance about the topic we want to mention and then look for openings. Visualize the opening, such as when the lead at the meeting asks if there is anything else to cover. We can then say, "Yes, I have something to share," and then share what we prepared. The more we envision this scenario in finer detail, the more it becomes embedded in us, and the more likely we are to carry out the envisioned scenario.

Changing our behavior to this new, envisioned future can cause fear. We are putting ourselves into a potentially uncomfortable situation because it is out of the ordinary for us. When we are fearful, we have chemical reactions in our bodies.[28] Hogue references several research studies that demonstrate the connection between our brains and the chemical reactions we have in our bodies.[29] When we experience feelings of fear, something is triggered in our brains, probably from our memories, and this trigger in turn sets off bodily reactions. These reactions produce chemicals, such as when there are states of fear we produce more cortisol. When these states are prolonged, the cortisol chemical can wreak havoc in our systems, destroying our natural balance. This, in turn, increases wear and tear on the body that can manifest in different types of illnesses. Oxytocin, on the other hand, is the chemical that the body produces when we have positive human interactions supporting good emotional development.

It behooves us to create these positive interactions when we are negotiating with others to build positive relationships. These experiences are stored as memories in the hippocampus, deep within our brains, and we continue to learn from them. The more ingrained our memories are, the stronger the pathways that are created. Recalling positive memories produces more oxytocin, further enhancing our positive emotional development. It is a positive cycle we wish to create and reproduce.

What to Expect in This Book

This book contains ideas about negotiation and approaches to get what we want. Some ideas center on strategies and tactics to achieve desired outcomes. Other ideas provide tips on what is needed to prepare, manage our emotions, deal with power differences, communicate effectively, and more. In this book, the approach to negotiation is based on a few principles, including those that frame negotiation as relational. The book's focus in negotiation is on the relationship between the engaged parties. It addresses personal and social narratives about women as negotiators and posits that the stories we carry with us support us in building quality relationships so that we are successful in our negotiations. It suggests identifying and changing the stories we carry that get in the way of successful negotiations. It also calls for nuances in negotiating, using the situation or context as a reference point to explore ideas about emotion when we are negotiating with family, and power when we are negotiating in the workplace.

Part 1 has three chapters that describe the stories by which we live. Chapter 1 is focused on building awareness of the stories we carry and their origins. It explores the role of culture and our social environments, how the stories, values, and beliefs we hold are formed, and how they influence our individual narratives about who we are. A key factor here is to develop more awareness about the stories we carry—how to enhance the ones that help us develop well and recognize those that get in the way of achieving the success we seek.

Chapter 2 explores the ways in which the latest thinking in neuroscience shows that these stories we carry and the language we use even in our inner dialogues shapes our brains. These patterns form pathways in our brains, which create the patterns of behavior. The idea of neuroplasticity, the malleability of the brain, suggests that we can effect lasting change in the stories we tell ourselves about who we are as negotiators and how those stories shape our negotiating performance.

Chapter 3 addresses issues of identity and explores why some of our beliefs "stick" and are harder to change than others. These stories are more central to who we are and our belief systems; there is more attached to them and thus more resistance to change. Part of the challenge here is that these stories are attached to our core beliefs of who we are and have been. Changing these stories has a ripple effect throughout our lives. It feels riskier to change these stories because of our deep attachment to them.

Part 2 has five chapters that focus on the context of the negotiation. Chapter 4 explores negotiating in the workplace. The concept of thinking of the workplace as a system is introduced, as are the dynamics inherent to systems and unique to the one in which we work. In particular, power dimensions are explored, and these ideas about power affect how we show up for and perform in our negotiations. Ideas about different sources of power are explored to expand our understanding of power from the typical "power over" stance.

Chapter 5 considers the family system. There are both generic family dynamics and those unique to our own family. The theme of identity, explored in Chapter 3, is expanded in this chapter to include ideas about the role of emotions, since our family relationships, which are formative, are also where and how we developed our emotional capacities and intelligence.

Chapter 6 explores our personal friendships and romantic relationships and how they affect us in our negotiations. They can be the place where we find our greatest strengths and vulnerabilities, all in the same relationship. These strong interpersonal connections can work in our favor, but at the same time, because the quality of our relationships is so key, we may tend to sacrifice achieving fulfillment in getting what we want because we deeply value the relationship and will sacrifice our outcomes for it.

Chapter 7 addresses the variety of situations in which we find ourselves negotiating. Examples include those where we don't have strong relationships with whom we are negotiating, or "one-off" negotiations with people we may never encounter again. Although the people and actual negotiations may be isolated, our own ideas and feelings about ourselves and our emotions can be triggered and feed further into the story about who we are as negotiators. There may be situations where we are trying to prove ourselves and address some issues that are gnawing away at us that may show up in what otherwise may seem like a negotiation struggle over a trivial matter.

Chapter 8 takes on those awkward situations in which we need to negotiate for our own emotional and physical safety. Typically, they can occur when we negotiate with someone who is in a position of power over us, whom we rely on, and who we trust. There may be unwanted sexual overtones to them, they may compromise our integrity, and they may be uncomfortable to talk about openly with others, which feeds into the lack of foundational support we need.

Part 3 has four chapters that put the ideas of the first two parts into practice. Chapter 9 covers preparing for the changes we want to make in becoming more effective negotiators. This chapter outlines the different steps we can take toward changing our narrative about who we are as negotiators so that we can develop new and enhanced tactics that will change our brain patterns and behaviors. It will also help us focus on the different situations in which we negotiate and the different negotiating partners we encounter.

Chapter 10 focuses on the process part of the negotiation, when we implement what we put together in the preparation phase. We make modifications as we go along because what actually happens in a negotiation may differ from what we anticipated.

Chapter 11 covers the post-negotiation follow-up, the steps we take to ensure that what we agreed to during the negotiation is implemented. It is a way of further supporting the agreements because at the end of so many steps in a negotiation it is important to keep track of who is responsible for taking the lead on the agreements each party made. It also sets the stage for subsequent negotiations that may follow.

Chapter 12 focuses on planning a strategy to implement the concepts we learned in the book and the tools explored in Chapter 9. The ways in which we implement our new strategy are important, as well as the ways we build in rewards to keep us motivated and encouraged. The chapter guides us in setting up milestones along the way and recognizing when and how we are improving on our path as competent and successful negotiators.

Chapters 13 through 15 are case studies focused on different contexts. All three cases include background information; the preparation, process, and post-negotiation phases; and the outcomes for the characters. Chapter 13 is a case study focusing on workplace dynamics and what happens when there is an external hire working with an internal candidate who did not get the position. Chapter 14 follows two siblings and focuses on family dynamics when they need to plan for taking care of their aging parent. Chapter 15 focuses on what happens in a romantic relationship when there are different career opportunities for both partners.

Enjoy your journey.

PART 1

THE STORIES WE LIVE BY

1

The Stories We Tell

Priya looked at herself in the mirror of the ladies' room and adjusted her shirt and jacket, smoothed her skirt, and ran her fingers through her hair. "You can do this," she said to herself. However, the look on her face was more doubtful than the command in her head. She nodded at herself and turned to leave the ladies' room to walk down the hall to her boss's office. It was time for her annual performance review, and Priya wanted to negotiate for increased responsibilities for herself, with a promotion, a change in job title, and a raise. She had been at her job for 18 months, and she thought her performance was above average and that she had fulfilled her responsibilities well. She also had not heard any negative feedback about her performance, so she assumed she was well-positioned for this advancement.

As she sat in the chair opposite his desk, she listened as her boss gave her feedback on her performance. Priya was not listening fully to his words as she was busy being hypersensitive to her boss's facial expressions and body language. She started to feel that he doubted her effectiveness in her current role, and she began to lose confidence in what she wanted to say and how much she wanted to advocate for herself. If this was how he felt about her performance, then there was no way she would be able to convince him otherwise. The script in her head went from "You can do this" to "Oh no, I have so far to go."

One interesting insight about this interaction is that it really was not an interaction in the fullest sense of the word. To be considered an interaction, conversation between two people has to occur. Instead, Priya was in her head and having a full-blown conversation with herself; How much of what her boss said did she actually hear? The important parts of a performance review include learning more about how the evaluation was made, questioning for a deeper understanding, offering additional information to influence the outcome, and identifying ways to improve. However, this was not a true negotiation of performance between the two parties because Priya and her boss were having parallel monologues.

Think about how many times you have thought you were in a negotiation but were actually having a monologue with yourself.

Origins of Narratives

Where do our stories—the narrative of our lives—come from? The world we live in carries many stories that are communicated to us throughout our lives. From our families to our education, to our communities, to the society at large, these stories shape who we are.[1] Many of these stories are based on ideas about who we should be because of our gender classification. "Women should do this because this is what women do." What are the messages you received growing up about being a woman and how has this shaped how you interact with others in the world around you?

These social stories filter into our personhood and become integrated into our stories of self—our personal stories, the narrative by which we live. Seyla Banhabib claims that, "Narratives cannot have closure precisely because they are always aspects of the narratives of others; the sense that I create for myself is always immersed in a fragile 'web of stories' that I as well as others spin."[2] This quote reflects the ongoing interchange between us and our social worlds so that as long as we are living in the world we will continue to be influenced by the stories of others in our social environment, and we will continue to influence others' stories as well.

Sometimes it is difficult to see the stories we carry until we are in a situation where our story is being challenged or doesn't fit. It is almost like being a fish out of water. The fish does not know it is in the water until it is out of it and recognizes the comfort and survival needs that are met by the water. Our stories, both social and personal, provide us with that same comfort and survival mechanism until we become aware that some of these stories may actually be getting in our way of being the best we can be.

Victoria Chen[3] makes note of the connections that exist between our personal and social/historical stories. There are different ways for us to probe and dig down to find our stories. She recommends using something called *systemic questioning* as a way of uncovering the implicit assumptions we have been carrying in our stories and to make explicit something that has been governing us our whole life.[4] We are part of multiple systems at any given time, such as home, family, work, community, and so on.

Systemic questioning "invites transparency, openness, connectivity, and critical reflection"[5] and can be used alone or with others. It provides a process for us to explore the origins of some of the beliefs we hold and how these beliefs became part of our story. When done with others it allows us to see where we stand and provides opportunities to develop shared meaning. It also provides us the chance to modify the aspects of our story that are not working for us. First, we need to make our story explicit and to notice what it contains and how it influences us before we will be able to change it.[6]

For our own story:

- How did I arrive at this particular understanding of this issue?
- Whose voices do I hear in my story?
- What has surprised me the most in this understanding of my story?
- How would things be different if I changed some aspects of my story?

In conversation with someone else:

- What are the similarities/differences in our stories?
- Whose voices are present/not present in our stories?
- What are the assumptions we are both making in these stories?[7]

Stories and Negotiation

Brené Brown[8] talks about the difference between perfectionism and wanting to advance and be better at whatever we do.[9] Perfectionism can be a trap and when we do not meet the criteria we set for ourselves, we end up feeling worse than we did before. This becomes the story of who we are and that story cycles around in our heads and plays out each time we try to do something new. Brown defines perfectionism as a "self-destructive and addictive belief system."[10] When we think of it in those terms, we can see that nothing good comes from it. When we set up unattainable goals and continue to strive for them and berate ourselves every time we fail in achieving what is not achievable, we feel shame, ridicule, and depression about ourselves and our prospects. Think about how this might affect us in our negotiations if we only focus on unattainable outcomes.

Priya's Story Revisited

Reflect on the monologue in Priya's head and her experience in her boss's office. Perhaps she was relying on perfection, wanting to get it right, rather than being attuned to what her boss was really saying. She went into that space of being self-critical and judgmental instead of listening to understand and questioning the comments her boss made. In fact, she was so clouded over with self-judgment, the old story of "you are not good enough, not experienced enough" occupied all her attention.

Unfortunately, much of this framing of perfectionism comes from cultural influences about the way girls and women should behave, especially the notion of women as nurturing types who take care of others.[11] The story is that if we are to be good girls and women, we advocate for others and not for ourselves; otherwise, we will be considered selfish, and that is not what we want to be. We are social beings, and we can appreciate the enormous task our families, schools, and communities have of educating us to be constructively contributing members of society. However, the tendency of these institutions is to perpetuate the familiar norms and gender roles regardless of whether we like it, feel it is a fit for how we identify, or believe it perpetuates a just world and one in which we can shine and grow. There is an inherent and biological view of survival we follow that promotes a resistance to change because we are suited to maintain the status quo.

A New Perspective

More recent orientations to examining gender—part of the nature versus nurture argument—have been shifting away from an essentialist perspective where men do this and women do that in clearly prescribed roles that result from our biology. Instead, we are moving toward a socially constructed view of gender, building on the influences of nurture that embraces a more complex view of the sexes and how that view has been shaped.[12] Deborah Kolb[13] explores the differences in these phenomena and acknowledges that while there are innate individual and gender-specific differences in behaviors, these are influenced by the social world around us.[14] The roles we play and the cultures of the institutions of which we are part have a big influence on how strong or weak they are in fostering gendered behavior.[15]

As Kolb and others explain, we take in the stories that exist in the social world around us about how we should behave, what we should say, and how we should say it. These stories from our social world nurture our beliefs and behavior. Barbara Czarniawska[16] talks about how societies determine the legitimate stories that set the moral high ground for what should be. This guides us in choosing to follow the stories that are deemed legitimate by our culture. Then, as individuals, we compare who we are in relation to this legitimate social story to see where we stand. We receive feedback from the world that informs us as to whether we are living in alignment with the dominant cultural story, or not. In turn, we also affect the world around us by our behavior; Are we going along as expected? Or are we making waves in an otherwise orderly system? The stronger the system around us, the less of an impact we make in upsetting the well-crafted status quo of what should be.

This back and forth between us and the world can be defined as communication and is not done in isolation. It is relational[17] and part of the process of how we make meaning together.[18] One of the main purposes of communication is to create an understanding between parties to satisfy needs. For example, we may need to know more about our environment so that we know our level of security. We may need information to decide on a joint or singular course of action. We may just want to connect with others to satisfy our social need for integration.[19]

As part of our human development, we need to shift from "I" to "we" if we want to have healthy social relationships.[20] It is a natural part of our brain's development and a necessary part of being integrated into our social worlds.

In terms of effective ways in which these goals of communication can be achieved, it is helpful to move away from the more traditional sender-receiver, or transmission model of communication because that style puts more of the onus on us as individuals when our lives are spent in relationship with one another.

Negotiation as a form of communication is a relational activity. In the transmission model of communication, we create (encode) a message as best we can, in isolation, and send it to the receiver, hoping that person understands (decodes) it the way we intended. There is a lack of regard for the space between our fuller self, who embodies multiple personas, such as being daughters, sisters, friends, mothers, colleagues, musicians, athletes, and so on. All of these personas we embody interact in the world around us and influence the messages we create and how they are understood. In a relational model of communication, we consider the meaning-making process from our own perspectives as well as try to gauge the perspectives of the other person with whom we are communicating. If we are trying to both understand and be understood, then we need to develop different types of awareness and knowledge of what that means and how it is influenced.

Gadamer[21] claims that we start out with our own prejudice because we frame our understanding from our own perspective before expanding it in conversation with others. It is through discourse or dialogue that we become more fully informed and then can expand our frames of reference and lessen our tendencies toward prejudice.[22] We need to incorporate the other's perspectives or we will not generate effective communication.[23]

A Communication Perspective

We can refer to the orientation just introduced as taking a communication-perspective approach to our interactions with others. Arthur Jensen[24] identifies four characteristics of a communication perspective that include looking at:

- the process of how we communicate, rather than at the intended outcome of our communication;
- communication from a meta-perspective so we can pay more attention to how we engage, such as our tone, behavior, and non-verbal gestures;
- what emerges in the conversation from our being together in this communication;
- how the stories we live are a part of ongoing stories that we share with others as we co-create our social worlds.

The relational aspect is that instead of being alone in our own heads about what should be and holding parallel monologues as Priya did in her performance evaluation, we are instead attuned to what we are making together. In other words, we are paying attention on so many levels (emotionally, nonverbally, conceptually what is not being voiced), and our contributions to the conversation are in response to others.

If we can pause for a minute to appreciate the atmosphere being created by this stance toward communication, then we can also see how negotiation is a relational communication process. It is an exchange between two persons in the same conversational space trying to bring some sense of mutual understanding and perhaps agreement with one another. We are co-creating a relational dynamic in this negotiation, perhaps one that will be part of an ongoing conversation we have with each other and, at a minimum, one that we will carry with us to our other negotiations.

The legitimate social stories that Czarniawska looked at of who we should be in the world influence us and help to create the personal narratives by which we live. These are the stories that cultures imbue in members to communicate values and the morals of what is right and what is wrong. These are the stories we learn from early childhood in our families, in school, and in all the social groups in which we participate. It creates a collective consciousness and narrative about the way the world should be and the way we should behave in that world. Czarniawska[25] also mentions that because of these social interactions, we are not the sole authors of our own narratives. There is a strong relational component in that we are always positioning ourselves in relation to the person with whom we are communicating. We make a statement, take a stance, and then how it is responded to by the other person in conversation determines whether it was accepted, rejected, considered, modified, questioned, and so on. In turn, we then respond to the other person's response to us, and a conversation flows. This can be done verbally as well as nonverbally.

An important consideration here is about our mindset and the mindset of the other person and how we need to coordinate across mindsets so that we are creating shared understanding.[26] We also need to consider the context, the space and climate of where we are communicating, in addition to the subject matter or content of our communication. These are all critical considerations in a negotiation. Are we in the office with our boss? Are we at home with our spouse or children? Are we at the grocers? All these contexts have set expectations of how we behave and interact with others, and we either fit in or don't. We will have a deeper look at contexts in chapters four through eight.

A useful framing for all this complexity inherent in our communication is a practical theory that takes a communication perspective, as mentioned by Jensen earlier, called *coordinated management of meaning* (CMM).[27] CMM is based on a triumvirate of principles to consider: *coordination, coherence,* and *mystery.*[28] The principle of coordination plays out in that during the course of any communication we are trying to coordinate meaning with the other person. We want to frame our communication so that we are understood by the other person in the way we intended. Likewise, we want to understand them in the way they intended.

There is much to consider here and a lot to juggle at the same time. We have intentions, thoughts, and feelings we hold onto, and at the same time we try to be attuned to the intentions, thoughts, and feelings of the other person. Additionally, we have these stories about who we are and how we feel about our own sense of competence that potentially cast doubt on us and affect our very ability to engage effectively. I am often amazed anyone communicates effectively at any time when we take all of these factors into consideration!

During our conversation with others, we're trying to create shared understanding in our meaning-making process. The basis of all communication is to coordinate the creation of shared understanding. If we succeed, then we have *coherence,* the second of three principles of CMM. Having a strong sense of coherence implies that the meaning we make together in coordination is in alignment with how we see the world, and that strengthens our sense of self and our identity. This feels good because we feel we are "in sync" with others.

If there is a lack of alignment and there are contradictory messages, then we may experience dissonance and lose the sense of coherence we seek. In many cases, when we are feeling dissonance and not strong in our own sense of self, it is difficult for us to be in coordination with others because we are not sure of ourselves, and then we might wonder if any coordination is taking place. This uncertainty increases feelings of self-doubt and will cloud judgment for effective communication to take place.

An example of this could be:

> You make an offer to help someone on his assignment. He responds with, "No, I can do it."
>
> You can understand that to mean:
>
> "Thank you for your help, but I do not want to feel obligated to you."
>
> "Thank you for your help, but do not insult me by implying I cannot do it."
>
> "Thank you for your help, but I know you are also busy."
>
> "Thank you for your help, but I need to learn how to do this on my own."

There are so many ways to interpret the response to your offer—and we have not even touched upon your intention in making the offer in the first place or the previous relationship you have with this person! All of this can influence the interaction and the meaning of the offer and response.

The world being the layered and complex place that it is means that there is a lot of ambiguity in our everyday lives. This is *mystery*, the third CMM principle. There is a great deal of the unknown in our world, and no matter how familiar a person or topic is, there is always the chance that new information or an unexpected outcome will come forth. We live in a dynamic space and time, and while we may prepare as best we can for what is to come there is always a chance that it will not go according to plan. How many times has that happened to you?

When the unexpected happens, we may lose our sense of balance because we were surprised at the turn of events, and it may take us time to recalibrate and make decisions about our next steps. If we are unprepared and do not have the agility needed to bounce back quickly, then we lose coherence of who we are in the world, because it is not moving along as we expected. We also may lose the coordination of being in sync with others because now we are out of sorts with ourselves, and this feeling may carry into the relationship. These three CMM principles of coordination, coherence, and mystery interact with each other. When one is changed in some way, it may have a ripple effect on the others. That is the nature of dynamism in your life.

Priya's Story Again

How do these stories show up in our negotiations? Where to begin? Going back to Priya and the turmoil in her head, she did not spend time coordinating meaning-making with her boss because her own story of who she is and her own feelings of not being good enough overshadowed any potential coordination toward an agreed-upon outcome. She stopped herself from engaging in a negotiation because of that unhealthy story in her head. She also had a story about the boss and who she is in relation to the boss that undermined her thinking that she had a right to be in that conversation. When she left the ladies' room to negotiate with her boss, she did not question her right to do so. She assumed she had that right. However, once she sat in his office, she created a social distance between herself and the boss.

Maybe it was because of the atmosphere of being in her boss's office and the status she attributed to it. Maybe it was the expression on his face that she interpreted to be unwelcoming and judgmental. Maybe she began to think of her title and position in the organization and put more power distance between them. Whatever was running through her mind at that time blocked her from having an effective and meaningful conversation.

Shaping a Negotiation

Whose responsibility is it to create these healthier and mutually beneficial negotiations? The short answer is that we all hold some of the responsibility, but we may not know it. If we continue down this line of thinking then there are a variety of ways in which to respond. One way is to think that we do not have sufficient power in the relationship to make a difference. I would counter that notion to agree that while we may not have all the *power* to make the final decision, there are ways we can *influence* it. We may say that we do not know how, that we do not have the skills—and I agree that there is always more to learn about being more effective in our negotiations. The good news is that there are skills and concepts that can be learned to make a difference and be better at getting what we need.

We have some sense of agency to influence what happens in our negotiations. We may feel burdened with the responsibility of managing our own destiny. Yes, it is a responsibility, and it can be daunting at times to consider this weight. We can also welcome knowing that we can guide our own journey in this life so that we get more of what we need in our interactions with others. At the same time, we are making the social worlds within which we live. So, while we are making the world a better place for ourselves, we need to make it better for others at the same time.

That is what it means to be in a relationship with others in negotiation. The process creates the fertile ground for our next negotiation and defines what our relationship will be like going forward. Negotiation is not only about the outcome, but about the process we take in getting *to* that outcome. And, when multiplied, our one-on-one negotiations equal our social worlds. We have probably experienced this already. If someone comes to us to negotiate competitively and beats us down to get everything they want, they are expressing what they have learned and experienced in other negotiations.

If we enter into a negotiation with a competitive mindset and behave competitively, there is going to be a competitive outcome with a winner and loser.[29] On the other hand, if we enter into a negotiation with the intention to collaborate with the other party and we do act collaboratively, then there is a better chance that there will be collaborative outcomes. The process determines the outcomes.[30]

We carry our experiences with us, and they affect every behavior and subsequent interaction we have. That is why framing a negotiation as being one part of a multi-turn process in the course of our lives puts it into perspective. We can think of negotiation as a "one-off"—something that occurs with that specific person about that particular issue. At the same time, the effects of the negotiation live on in us, in the other person, and in the world around us because those effects influence what we think, say, and do in all other interactions that follow. So, even when we are having a seemingly different negotiation with a different person about different issues, the stories we tell ourselves about who we are as negotiators cause us to bring every negotiation with us into the next.

In this chapter, we explored how the narratives we live by are formed by our social worlds, and how we, in turn, *influence* our social worlds. Language and communication play an important role in shaping our behavior, which includes how we communicate and behave while preparing for and engaging in negotiation. In the next two chapters, we will explore how language affects our brains and how the brain waves we create affect our behavior. And we will see why some of the changes we want to make in our brains and behaviors are more challenging than others, especially when the behaviors are wrapped up in our identity.

Reflection Questions

1. What are the stories you tell yourself about how you negotiate?
2. Which stories are helpful? Which get in the way of you being more confident, more assertive, more successful?
3. What are the major influences that shape these stories in your narrative?

2

How Words Affect Our Brains

Tammy was beginning to feel the frustration that typically came along when she had conversations with one of her co-workers. She could not understand why he could not understand what she was asking him to do. He attended the same team meetings as she did, and he heard the same directions that she did, but, for some reason, he could not follow them. When Tammy, as team leader, would follow up with him to assign an action plan based on the information gleaned from the meeting, she was amazed at his lack of shared understanding.

She knew that when she became short-tempered, it only led to more frustration and bad blood between them. She could not find the patience to explain the assignments to him and did not think it was her responsibility. He was an adult and he needed to figure it out. Their conversations never seemed to end well. They followed the same disastrous patterns, and she often told herself not to "go there" even as she was saying the words she knew she could not take back.

Language is an important part of our lives and the basis of our communication. On any typical day, we are not usually conscious of each word we use except when we are faced with the challenge of communicating with someone whose beliefs are different than ours and who frames communication differently than us. We often do not know what we do not know until faced with a situation that differs from what we expected. It is only then that we become aware that we were operating under a particular set of assumptions that differed from those of our conversation partner—assumptions we did not even realize we were making.

It can be unnerving when this happens because we prepared for a particular flow in our communication that was redirected in a way we had not anticipated. We may not consciously notice this turn in the conversation and think it is just a misunderstanding. In this case, we push harder at what we are saying or doing because we are stuck in our own patterns and beliefs. If we say it loudly enough or more assertively, surely the other person will hear it!

Alternatively, we may think the other person did not get what we were saying the first time, and we repeat what we said or did, thinking the other person will now understand. Or we believe they are wrong, and our mission shifts from getting them to see our point of view to getting them to see the errors of their ways, which we will correct. A much rarer response may be that we are puzzled by this different response, and our curiosity rises to prompt us to explore the basis of these differences.

Habits and Learning

Miscommunication shows up in our negotiations as well. We have in mind that the flow will follow a prescribed pattern that we thought about away from the other person. When the response is not what we expected, any one of several of the responses listed above could happen. We have taken for granted assumptions about the way things should be because that is the way they have been according to the social scripts we've learned and by which we live. However, what we experience is that not everyone lives by the same social script. Here is where it could get threatening, frustrating or just plain interesting.

Many of us grew up hearing the saying, "You can't teach an old dog new tricks." In many cases, that turned out to be true as we learned certain habits and beliefs very well that we could rely on without any conscious effort. It means that the socialization and education practices of our homes, communities, and schools were effective in bringing us into the world and our societies to be properly functioning adults in those contexts. Socialization creates patterns for us in our lives that we are probably unaware of unless we try to notice them or have them thrust on us, throwing us off balance, as in the fish out of water scenario. In many instances, these patterns of what we believe and how we behave serve us well and satisfy us. In other cases, however, they actually block us from living fuller, richer lives.

Part of the old saying about not being able to learn new tricks is that there was and still is a widespread belief that once we reach a certain age or level of developmental maturity, that's it, no more serious learning takes place. We can pick up a few things along the way, like memorizing certain expressions in a foreign language, but becoming fluent in that language is a much bigger, if not insurmountable, challenge.

Results of recent research about how our brains work provide evidence that our brains can be molded into new patterns of learning, known as *neuroplasticity*.[1] Think about the ability of plastic to be molded or reformed into new shapes; that view of the ability to be reshaped is being applied to our brains. You have possibly heard the expression that "neurons that fire together wire together" as a shorthand way of saying that you create these neural pathways leading to your habits by what you associate together. This is based on the Hebbian theory, which posits that the more you experience these associations, the more embedded they become in your brain, and the more quickly the association is made.[2] Thus, habits are formed. So, if you have a frightening experience with a dog, you may continue to feel fear when you see dogs.[3]

Memory and Associations

This idea of association can also be applied to what we think about and how we feel about negotiation. Maybe we have had a disappointing or even devastating experience in a negotiation. Because we felt like such a failure, every time we hear the word *negotiation* we become fearful and avoid it as much as possible. By avoiding engaging in negotiations and trying again, we build that bad experience up to be a bigger failure than it actually was.

This association is with us, and the deeper the emotional experience, the more embedded and visceral the memory. Every time we have a negotiation that mirrors that bad experience, we relive it, and it creates a stronger grip on our memory. The memory grooves become deeper, and it is more likely that we will continue to have those same negative associations.[4]

In our brains, we are deepening and strengthening the neural pathways that hold our memories. Research shows that language and the choice of words we use—including our inner dialogue, our self-talk—creates and reinforces these neural pathways.[5] Research in the area of SDN, self-directed neuroplasticity (that is a mouthful!), shows that we can actually change the neural pathways in our brains.[6]

We can break down SDN into two steps. First, we need to unlearn the negative stories we associate with negotiating. That falls under the category of long-term depression, LTD. We need to replace those negative stories with positive, encouraging stories that frame more successful engagements in negotiation, with what is referred to as long-term potential, or LTP.[7] Because our brains are malleable, we can learn new stories by rewiring the neurons that fire together. This leads to new ways of being in the world by replacing the stories that hold us back with stories that are generative and provide us more growth opportunities.

Take a moment to reflect on this profound observation. The implications are that when we apply this idea to our efficacy at negotiating, we can change how we approach negotiations and the outcomes of our negotiations by changing the way we think about them. This is both liberating and scary because it shows us that we have so much power and responsibility all at the same time! With that power and responsibility comes the need for building our capacity so that the changes we make are positive and intentional. We do not want to make a change for the worse!

There are certain patterns we establish in how we think and speak about what we do. When it comes to negotiating, we have a preset script in our heads based on our past experiences. If we were successful in achieving the outcomes we wanted, then we feel we are competent. Our inner thoughts reflect these sentiments so that we tell ourselves, "I can do this. I got this. I know how to negotiate." Chances are high, however, that we often do not feel successful in getting what we want in our negotiations and our inner thoughts reflect those sentiments, telling us, "I am not good enough. I do not know what I want. I cannot negotiate."

Language and Plasticity

Words have an impact on us in several ways. Language and the words we use create thought, and these thoughts create the language we use. The language we use creates patterns in our brains.[8] When we tell ourselves we cannot do something, the neurons creating those pathways are strengthened. If we tell ourselves we cannot negotiate, whenever we approach a negotiation, we will associate failure with the process and outcomes. As mentioned above, neuroplasticity postulates that "neurons that fire together wire together." In other words, we have wired negotiation and failure together.

However, if we reframe the process of engaging in the negotiation and what we define as a successful outcome, we have a chance to rewire our neurons to create different pathways. For example, if we set our intention of being more thorough in our preparation, and then we actually are, we have now set up a new pattern for success. We have wired negotiation preparation with success and created a new neural pathway. If we reward ourselves for even making the effort, regardless of how challenging it is or how fearful we are, even if the outcomes we set are not achievable, we pair effort and success together in a new neural pathway.[9]

The bottom line is that we have agency in the neural pathways we create and the language we use. Self-directed neuroplasticity reflects the power of our thoughts to create new neural pathways in our brains. What we think creates patterns in our brains that influence our behavior. This means that we need to be more intentional in what we think because we need to limit our fear-based thoughts that, in turn, limit our development and progress. To succeed, we must replace fear-based, negative thoughts with generative wording that encourages us to move forward in positive ways.[10] We can do this!

Tammy's Story Revisited

If we revisit the conversation Tammy was having in her head about her co-worker and apply some of what we have learned about patterning, we can see that Tammy has developed a habit in her communication. Even though she told herself not to go there, she went there because there is a strong neural pathway that was established over time. However, brain plasticity will allow Tammy to learn new habits and patterns of communication. First, she will need to manage her frustration. If she is in that emotional state, she will not bring her best self forward. Then she needs to think of a suitable alternative.

One way Tammy can address her co-worker's seeming confusion is to open a line of inquiry with him to better understand what needs clarification. Asking open questions is a good start. Tammy will need to have a good mindset and the desire to engage in this unlearning and relearning process. Then she must practice so that these new pairings of neurons have chances to fire and then wire together. She will need to also reward herself for small improvements—even if it is just counting to ten before responding—to give her new communication patterns a chance to kick in. Tammy now has a plan to move forward to change her relationship dynamics with her co-worker and to create a better work environment for all.

Mindfulness

One way to handle fear-based thoughts is to be mindful of what we say and think. Mindfulness practices, many of which are based on very old traditions, have been given more attention recently. Mindfulness practices focus our attention and block out distractions that decrease our concentration. Our focus puts energy into what we want to grow. It is useful to practice mindfulness so that when it is needed during other interactions, it can be called upon and used effectively. It is not wise to start a mindfulness practice when in the middle of a difficult emotional experience.

We can equate mindfulness with muscle memory, as in dancing. When we hear the beat of a certain rhythm, we automatically remember the steps and movements associated with that beat because we have practiced them enough to internalize the movements into our muscles. These memories are triggered when we hear the music. We have conditioned our body to dance, and we can condition our minds to focus when we apply mindfulness to creating new neural pathways to aid us in being more effective in our negotiations.

Reframing and Plasticity

Another useful approach to changing the patterns in our brains, our behavior, and the outcomes of our negotiations is through the practice of reframing. It is a typical habit for us to comment on what did not work well when we are finished with a project, activity or negotiation rather than focus on what went well. Whatever we focus on grows because we are putting our attention there and feeding it energy. If we look for problems, we will find problems. Instead, if we look for what is working well, we will find multiple examples of small and large success points.[11]

An example of this is commending yourself on even putting in the effort to try and negotiate for what you want. This new pairing of rewarding your effort and not focusing only on the outcomes you did not receive or the fact that you felt you choked up when challenged helps you stick to reframing the experience into a positive one. The more you engage in this positive reframing, the stronger the ability to continue because you make it a habit and wire your neurons accordingly.[12]

Constructive Substitute

To change the patterns of behavior from those that result in unwelcome outcomes to those that foster constructive negotiations, we need to have other behaviors in mind that substitute for the less helpful behaviors. We can be creatures of habit, and even if we know that what we are about to say or do will not bring us what we want, we still say it and do it anyway. How many times have you told yourself, "Don't go there," and yet you still go there? This is the situation that Tammy found herself in when she repeated the response pattern she developed when reacting to her frustration with her co-worker.

There is a sense of agency because the opposite would be helplessness, and we know we must do something. However, we repeat the same behaviors because that is what we know and that is what is familiar. On one hand, we really need to commend our brains on how marvelously efficient they are in pushing us forward into familiar territory, even if the results are not what we want. Efficiency wins over alternative processes and outcomes that are new, less familiar, and, therefore, less efficient.[13]

To start, envision the desired outcome, accompanied by a new and honed set of skills that will support this newly envisioned outcome becoming a reality. It is really important in changing any behavior that there is an intention to do so supported by motivation.[14] Our brains resort to the behavioral patterns with which we are familiar, as these neural pathways are already formed, and the brain expends less energy in following what is established. It takes a concerted amount of attention to shift from what *is* to what you *want to be* because new pathways need to be formed.[15] It is too easy to fall back on spending less energy, which means relying on old habits and patterns. It takes diligence to make change happen.

To stay motivated, it is important that we think of ways to reward ourselves so that we support the creation of the behavioral patterns we want and foster the outcomes we desire. We need to be realistic and break down our efforts into smaller, bite-size chunks so that we increase our possibilities of success. It may sound illogical, but it often happens that we imagine the total end result and set ourselves up for failure because we are unrealistic about what we can accomplish. We are going from zero to one hundred, completely jumping over all the steps along the way. We need to break it down into small and attainable steps in order to keep up the momentum of change. Then we can reward ourselves along the way at every step and achievement. These small gains, when collected together, will be big leaps. Setting up the big leaps, to begin with, is difficult to achieve and sustain. We want to maintain whatever change we foster, allowing for a little slippage every now and again.

An example of small steps we can take in preparation for an upcoming negotiation:

- Set the date for the negotiation
- Begin your preparation by reviewing the steps for negotiation preparation (see Chapter 9)
- Gather the materials for your preparation
- Begin sketching out a strategy for the long-term goals
- Identify the role this negotiation plays in your long-term strategy

- Identify your strengths and prepare your pep talk
- Identify what you want to watch out for (know your triggers) and identify ways to compensate for them
- Practice with someone and ask for feedback
- Integrate the feedback into your approach
- Remember to congratulate yourself for engaging

Breaking this preparation process down can allow us to continue to be motivated because we are making small accomplishments along the way. This will boost our morale and give us that added strength to engage in the negotiation.[16]

Strengthen New Neural Pathways and Weaken Maladaptive Ones

I mentioned earlier that what we pay attention to grows because we are giving it energy and life. This also implies that what we *do not* pay attention to withers and dies. If any of us has ever kept plants, we know that attention and love help plants grow and thrive. When we leave them for a week of travel, we are not sure what we may come back to, and if they have not completely left this world, we may have to tend to them carefully to bring them back to life again. The same applies to behaviors we do not want. In this case, we *do* want the old behaviors to wither away and leave us. As we continue to give energy to the new behaviors and take the previously allotted energy away from the old behaviors, we allow ourselves space and time to become tired because we are making concerted efforts at change.

Remember that our brains are looking for the path of least resistance and that path includes the familiar patterns. We need to reward ourselves for the small gains we make each time we make the effort, and these efforts need to be often and consistent so that we can create these new neural pathways and stay motivated.[17]

Once again, we really need to commend those around us who have continued to teach us how to be in the world, what to believe, and how to act. When we are young, it works well to believe that people have good intentions, and they are doing the best they can with what they know and what they can do. Then we become adults and we carry stories that permeate every aspect of our lives about who we are and what is right and wrong. The good news is that we can recognize these stories for what they are and then take steps to do things differently if what we are doing is not serving us well. It also means we accept that we are responsible for making the changes we want. If the social narratives we carry do not work, then we must make efforts to change them.

Sometimes we do things that are not helpful and might even be hurtful, and we need to slow down, even stop, and ask ourselves where this idea came from and why we continue doing what is not helpful. If what we are doing gets in the way of being effective in our negotiations, we need to question why we are continuing to sabotage ourselves. Yes, it takes a lot of time and energy to make changes, and making change can be very uncomfortable. Yet doing the same things over and over again without positive results is also uncomfortable because it keeps us from performing well and achieving what we have earned and deserve.

It is a choice we must make about where we want the discomfort. Do we want it to be in the same unhelpful patterns of our thoughts, communication, and behavior that do not lead us to our desired outcomes? Or do we want the discomfort to be in learning new patterns of thought, communication, and behavior that could lead us to something more constructive, positive, and generative? The expression "no pain, no gain" applies; change can be painful, but we can lessen the pain if we keep a positive mindset that the result will be beneficial and give us energy.

We've explored how intertwined our brains and neural

pathways are with our language, communication, and behavior. One influences the other in a repetitive cycle. For example, changes in how we communicate, including our word choices, result in changes in the neural pathways in our brains. This, in turn, affects how we choose to act in the moment, and these behaviors then influence our brains and communication as well, and the cycle continues. The more deeply embedded any of these habits are, the more challenging it will be to change them. Change is usually uncomfortable, but when we intentionally change for improvement, the results do feel better.

Reflection Questions

1. What are some of your favorite approaches to your mindfulness practice?
2. What behavior would you like to modify or what new behavior would you like to develop? How might you make it happen?
3. What are some of the ways you can keep yourself motivated to pursue the changes you want to make?

3

Stories That Stick

It all leads back to her third-grade school performance when she felt sick and vomited in the staircase on the way to the stage. Too embarrassed to do anything else, Birgitta continued on with the rest of her class and performed. She felt the need to carry through with the role assigned her and didn't feel she had any other options.

When she told her mother about the incident after the show, her mother said, "That's my girl. The show must go on." That comment alone impacted Birgitta, and since that time, she perseveres because she is the one who gets things done. She does not want to let anyone down or become known as the one who stopped the show.

There are many stories we grow up with that stay with us, while others fade away or change. What is it about these stories that gives them the ability to stick with us, wanted or not? For example, we can be teased as being awkward during the preadolescent years, and, even though we may have become graceful adults, that awkward person story stays with us.

In Chapter 1, we explored how stories are formed from our social situations and our personal experiences. As part of a social system, we also identify with particular groups, and our affinities with these groups shape our identity. Perhaps we belonged to certain groups—such as being part of math club or cheerleading—and these affiliations stimulated particular behaviors in us. Behaviors associated with these stories of us as members of those groups are replicated into patterns, creating in our brains tried and true pathways leading to predictable behaviors as explored in Chapter 2, and the cycle continues.[1] In that chapter, we explored how neurons that fire together wire together and become embedded as neural pathways in our brains.[2]

The stories that stay with us are intertwined, creating our identity. Changing these stories could mean a radical shift in our own belief systems because we are changing the stories that are central to our core being. For example, if we belonged to a math club when we were young but later had negative experiences with math (perhaps we performed poorly in an advanced calculus class) perhaps we now doubt our competence in math. This represents a change to one of our main stories of who we are. Noticing these significant changes in our identity can be a very unsettling experience.[3] Everything we experienced and understood about the world and our place in it is in accordance with who we believe we are. We believed we were a math whiz and understood the world from this familiar perch. An alteration in this aspect of our identity can cause us to rethink all interactions and experiences we have had in the past. We do not trust our judgment. It means our self-image is changing, followed by changes in our behaviors and how we interact with others.

This is almost like someone pulling the rug out from under us—everything becomes topsy-turvy. All that we understand about the world around us comes under scrutiny because the frames of reference we used in the past were different. This shift in perception can cause us to question and even doubt ourselves and our judgment. Our identity and sense of self comes into question.

Another example can be that we may have been a star performer and achieved excellence in our younger years and schooling. Then we secured a position as a consultant in a top global firm, and now we work side-by-side with other top performers. We work on complex problems that need to be solved in innovative ways, and the answers are not coming easily or quickly. Perhaps for the first time we are feeling intellectually challenged in ways we never could have imagined. Doubts creep into our mind that were never there before, and we begin to question how smart we really are. We wonder if we were smart in other situations or if they were easy wins and now our true competence is coming under scrutiny. We rethink other assumptions and almost everything is fair game for questioning.

This, of course, has implications for the others with whom we interact. If we change our responses to them, they can no longer continue to give us their same responses. If we believe that we develop our sense of self in interactions with others because it is a relational process, then changes in others could have a ripple effect to cause changes in us as well. On the other hand, their own beliefs about who they are, who we are, and who we are together may be strong enough to resist any type of change we may want to bring to the relationship. Now, we face resistance. Systems have a strong sense of wanting to maintain the status quo and efforts to change the current system will be met with a strong tug to keep it the same or put it back the way it was.

Systems and Story Creation

We live in systems—in our families, in our workplace, in our communities. "A system is an interconnected set of elements that is coherently organized in a way that achieves something."[4] Each system has three parts: *elements*, and in the case of stories these can be the people in the story, the events; *interconnections*, or relationships between the elements; and a *function or purpose*, the reason for the system doing what it needs to do to survive.[5]

Therefore, when we change our response in a situation, we change the dynamics that take place between us and the other person (the elements), sending ripples across the system. If others are open to these changes, then they will also change in response, depending on the strength of the shift and the impact. Systems can be resistant to change, and even with significant shifts, the tendency is for the system to revert to the status quo, the way it was before the disturbance.[6] This tendency is due to the feedback loops within the system that try to maintain the balance or status quo.[7] The pull of the familiar is so strong that even if the change is beneficial, the system will go back to the familiar patterns that were previously established.[8]

Part of what happens in our relationships within systems

is that we are sometimes labeled or give labels to others as shorthand ways of referring to an outstanding characteristic. Some of these labels are generative and aid us in living up to our potential, but other labels hold us back. Think about what happens to you when you are referred to as the smart one, the pretty one, the shy one, the slow one. Before you walk into the room, your identity attached to that label precedes you, and then whatever you say or do either confirms or refutes that label.

Perhaps you were known as the rebel in your family when you were young. You are now an adult and have been out on your own for a number of years. You are educated, you have a good job, yet the label of being a rebel sticks to you. Any comment you make that might not be considered mainstream confirms the label, even if you are not really challenging or contradicting anyone. You think you have moved past that label—that it belonged to a phase of your life from long ago. But some family members who do not see you on a regular basis and have not seen your growth and professional success are stuck in the story of the past.

We also help create and perpetuate the social stories we live in. There are several positive aspects to collective storytelling and story creation, because the telling of stories brings us into social bonds that fulfill our need to belong to a group,[9] to be part of a tribe.[10] Stories and their tellings also fulfill a core part of how humans are designed—with a need for social interaction and integration.[11] The interaction between our personal story development and the social story creation of which we are a part are woven together and influence one another.

To illustrate this point, we may enjoy being affiliated with a group that supports sustainability of the environment. It is a positive association and aimed toward the social good. We therefore sacrifice our Saturday mornings to join group clean-up efforts, like picking up trash in a local park or collecting recyclable materials. It connects us to others who share this affiliation, and it feeds into our own individual story of being a good person, considerate of others and the earth.

This need for social bonding influences our identity, and our identity, in turn, increases our social bonding in the groups with which we identify.[12] Our identity is strengthened by our narrative about ourselves and our group membership. It helps us make sense of the social world we live in and how to be a positive member of the group. The group continues to write its narrative, and we as members of the group join in the co-creation process. There are several benefits of this process of co-constructing a shared narrative as members of a particular identity group. The narratives help the group members deal with the mystery and ambiguity of life,[13] it reinforces social bonds, and it maintains group cohesion by also differentiating what the group is not.[14]

Identity Groups

Identity groups often carry labels that can be welcome if we want to be identified with a particular label. But especially when we do not choose the identity group with which we are associated, we may be influenced to accept the grouping fully or with some reservations, or to deny, not acknowledge, and even resent the identification. The affiliation assumes a relationship with other members of that same identity group whether we experience a level of familiarity personally, or whether it is assumed we have a strong similarity that is placed on us by external sources. "They are of this group, therefore, they must all think/feel/act this way."[15]

This is when stereotypes come into play. If we are born into a certain culture, then those external to that culture may place stereotypical attributes on us, such as, "They are from X culture; therefore, they are indirect communicators" or

"Those people are very emotional when they speak." People from within the same culture may also make assumptions that we know and follow the norms of the culture we share, and they will expect certain types of behavior from us. Perhaps the culture is one that defers to elders and accepts their decisions because voicing a different opinion would be considered disrespectful.

Some of these affiliations we are born into, and others we voluntarily join. In other cases, we are placed in groups and identified as members of those groups by others who hold more power than we do. If we are associated with a particular group that we do not want to be a member of for some reason, we upset the status quo when we try to make a change. For example, as women we are assigned certain characteristics and ways of being in the world that we do not want to sustain because those traits do not work well for us and may hold us back. It is good to reflect on these associations placed on us as women and consider how this shows up in our negotiations. For example, consider the notion that women do not speak up and advocate for themselves. This does not work well for us because we are ambitious and believe we have good contributions to make, yet we are not being called on to participate. We need to assert ourselves into conversations to make our contributions and be heard. We accept the categorization of being a woman, but we don't accept all the attributes associated with it.[16]

These beliefs about how we should be in the world may manifest in stories that are told *by* members of the group or by external parties *about* members of the group. Typically, within groups there is a higher level of detail and knowledge about the group and its members. These stories are more nuanced in their description, whereas external observations are less granular and tend to be less precise. A reliance on stereotypes and attributions placed on members of a group is common. The messages in the stories may be subtle, such as the description of good wives being docile and following their husbands' lead. We are not being told directly that we should be docile and follow if we want to be considered good, yet this is what is being communicated to us.

We live and function in the world with different sets of expectations about how we can be safe and secure. We make assumptions about how others will behave, and this gives us a sense of safety and security because the more predictable our environment, the better prepared we can be in our encounters. Too much unknown causes uncertainty that can lead to insecurity because we do not know how we can be safe physically, emotionally, and psychologically. This is where the fight, flight or freeze response comes into play as a means of protection.[17] There is evidence that women responding to stress "tend and befriend" as a response to reduce risk.[18] This is based on the role women play in nurturing and caregiving and may be in alignment with women's protective nature to take care of their offspring.

Birgitta's Story Revisited

One of the stories Birgitta developed that became a core part of her identity was that she was dependable. Even if doing so caused great discomfort, she cannot imagine not being there to support others and fulfill her commitments. Asking for help at times is very challenging for her. She assumes everyone else knows she will be there to pick up the slack, and she believes that as well. This is who she is and how she expects the world to see her. She helps perpetuate the label of being dependable to others.

For her to make a change, she would first need to accept for herself that she is not perfect and see that it is okay to ask for help. This means, however, that she would need to shift her own sense of self and identity. Birgitta asking for help does not mean she is any less dependable. In fact, with a healthy reframe, it could be seen as further proof she is very dependable because she knows her limits and will still deliver, with the support of others.

Identity and Negotiation

In a negotiation context, the more predictable our negotiating partner's responses to us, the better able we are to guide the negotiation toward favorable outcomes. We know in advance with a good deal of certainty what our negotiating partner is likely to say, and we can plan our response. Here is where the importance of good and thorough preparation cannot be stressed enough. The better prepared we are, the better able we are to respond to different likely scenarios. When the flow of the negotiation changes and our negotiating partners take a turn different than expected, thorough preparation can also enable us to be more agile in the moment.

Our sense of identity provides information that affiliates us with those to whom we are similar and separates us from those who differ. If we think of negotiation as a relational activity, we are trying to figure out the ways in which we are similar to and different from our negotiating partner. This information is helpful in a number of ways and can be discovered during the preparation phase and confirmed during the actual negotiation. We want to know how to communicate effectively with the other party. The more we know and understand about them the better able we are able to tailor our communications, ensuring that they hear what we want to say in the way in which we intended.

Communication is a complicated and complex process, and there is no guarantee that what we say will be taken as we intended it, but the better we know the other person and the better our skills and capacity to formulate our communication the more likely we will be in coordination with one another. This comes partly from knowing the ways in which we are similar and different. How the other person identifies which affinity groups they belong to can also provide us with some of that information.

This is an important notion because we cannot assume that other people like or dislike what we do and that they want to hear what we have to say. Misunderstandings can occur if we expect a particular response that we do not get. We make assumptions on a regular basis, some of which may not be accurate. It is important to check our assumptions as we prepare for the negotiation, then continue to confirm or adjust them as needed.

When we see people of a particular gender, race, or ethnicity, we may make assumptions about how they negotiate, what is important to them, where their strengths and weaknesses can be found. In some cases, our assumptions may work in our favor because our assessment is accurate. However, it is risky to stay with those assumptions without further clarification as there is more variation than what is characteristic of a gender stereotype.[19]

When we explore the characteristics of our own identity groups, we gain a deeper look into our own sense of self. The more we know, the more we can ascertain how these characteristics influence us and how we can effectively live with these attributes. These are part of the social narratives that are imbued throughout our personal narratives. It is important to identify the origins of these beliefs and practices so we know why and how they came into being and a part of who we are.

An example of this is an exercise based on the *coordinated management of meaning*,[20] discussed in Chapter 1. This exercise is also described in greater detail in Chapter 9. To address it briefly now, draw a daisy flower, and in the center of the flower write your name (Figure 3.1). You can write more of a description after your name to reference in a bit more detail which aspect of yourself you are examining in more depth. If you want to know more about what it means to be a woman, you can write your name and "woman identity group." Then, on the petals surrounding the daisy, write the significant influences that shape your beliefs and identity as a woman. They can be people, places, events, from any time in your life that are meaningful to you at this moment.

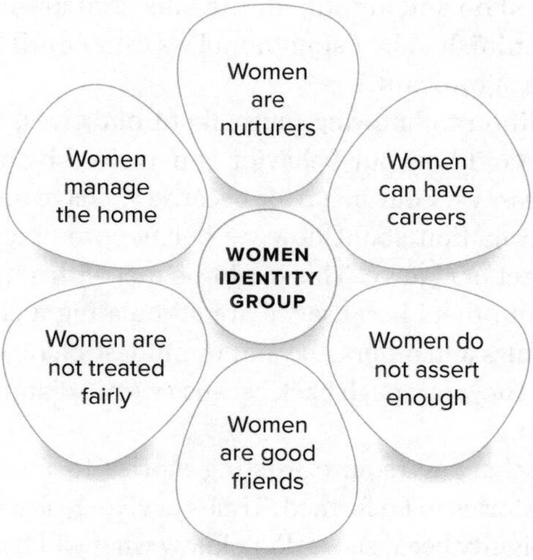

FIGURE 3.1 Daisy Model

The Daisy Model can be used to depict different identity groups with which women may identify. These identity groups usually have stories associated with them that may or may not be accurate for the individual. *Based on the Daisy Model used with permission by Cronen and Pearce in W. Barnett Pearce from* Making Social Worlds: A Communication Perspective *(Malden: Blackwell Publishing, 2007), p. 180; permission conveyed through Copyright Clearance Center, Inc.*

After you name the different influences, return to each petal and identify the ways in which they shape your behavior and beliefs about being a woman. Maybe your mother was a major influence, and you frame the messages your mother gave you about being a woman and the ways those messages show up today in your life. Or maybe it was an experience you had that left a strong impression on you. Identify the ways this experience shaped your beliefs about being a woman. After reflecting on each of the petals, you can also decide which influences help you be a better negotiator and which are getting in the way of your effectiveness. The ones that are helpful are focused on and amplified; the ones that are not helpful are diminished by using them less often until they become less significant.

In addition to knowing more about ourselves, we want to understand how our behavior is perceived by others. If we decide to vary our behavior because we have uncovered more information about how we behave, we may cause a ripple effect of change. This might be met with some resistance from others because we are stimulating a change in the dynamics and others may not want these changes thrust on them. They may push back because we are disturbing the status quo.

These changes require existing stories to be modified and new stories to be formed. Times of change are rampant with ambiguity because we don't know what will be. It is interesting that even when there is general agreement that the status quo is not satisfactory, people tend to resist changes to the very system they do not like.[21] On one level, it does not make any sense because change is what is needed and welcomed. However, on the other hand, the uncertainty about how change will affect us is so unsettling it causes us to shut down from an overload to the system that is trying to keep us psychologically and emotionally safe.

For those of us who have less tolerance for ambiguity, we try to settle our narratives and keep them steady as a way of increasing stability. However, as we live in social systems, exchanging perspectives and points of view with others, our narratives are susceptible to change. We are individual open systems that are part of larger social network systems, and the open borders cause information to pass back and forth. This exchange of information brings about changes in our perspectives, beliefs, and behaviors. If we are feeling unsafe in certain situations and do not feel comfortable sharing fully, we may emotionally edit ourselves so that we only share what is acceptable and safe to share. Being able to have a social network that allows for fuller sharing because of the safety net that comes from common ground, acknowledgement, and shared experiences is critical for our health and well-being.

In this chapter, we explored the different identity groups to which we belong: those we are born into, those we select, and those we are assigned to by others. There are stories we carry about what it means to be a member of these groups, some of which are constructive, while others get in the way of us being effective communicators and negotiators. We looked at using the lens of *coordinated management of meaning* to unpack the different layers and influences that shape our identity, such as applying the daisy model, to gain deeper insights into the several factors that make up who we are. These stories are a core part of our identities and, while not impossible, are more challenging to modify.

In the next section, we apply the foundations of what we explored in Part One to different contexts covered in Part Two. This includes and is not limited to how stories of self are formed, the relationship between our brains and our behavior, and how our identities are formed and nurtured.

Reflection Questions

1. What aspects of your identify make you especially proud? In what ways?
2. In what ways have you changed your narrative about your own identity groupings?
3. What assumptions have you made based on stereotypes you may hold? How do you think you might change those assumptions?

PART 2

CONTEXT MATTERS

4

Negotiating in the Workplace: Organizations as Systems

Soraya started a new job and was eager to show she was a team player. Her manager assigned her tasks to do that were outside of her job description, but she did them because she was a hard worker, wanted to perform well, and liked to learn. She believed it was the right thing to do. She also believed it would be temporary, but her manager continued to give her work outside her scope of responsibilities, and it became the norm rather than the exception. Through it all, Soraya did not question why her manager gave her these tasks. She continued to have regular meetings and did not question this extra work. She thought she would be setting herself up for success. However, this pattern continued for two years, and in the second year she began to realize that these extra assignments were not benefiting her professionally. She realized that she needed to negotiate better boundaries and stay on track for her own career development.

Much has been written, researched, and discussed about women being less effective at negotiations than men. Some conclusions are based on perceptions of power imbalance; others on stereotyped behavior, expectations or biases. However, more nuanced research shows that while in some cases women do underperform men, there are other times when they hold their own or even outperform their male counterparts.[1]

If we take a closer look at some of these perceptions as compared with performance outcomes, we can see there are different factors that influence how well a woman will perform in her negotiations in the workplace based on how well trained and experienced the woman is at negotiating. Studies have shown that the more experienced the woman negotiator, the better she performs and the better the outcomes of her negotiation are as compared to less experienced women.[2]

More experienced women negotiators are less negatively impacted by gender stereotypes. They have avoided the pitfall of shying away from a negotiation by framing it as "an ask."[3] There is something about the term *negotiation* that many women find off-putting, and they avoid engaging. Because women are more comfortable asking than telling, the framing of asking rather than negotiating suits them well.[4]

An example of this could be requesting something from a colleague because it is important to furthering the project. Framing it as a request for a project and not for oneself diminishes the likelihood that the request would become a point of contention in a negotiation scenario. Saying it is for the project and not oneself could also make it easier to claim value because it is for the team and organization, not one person.

Experienced women negotiators also use negotiations as opportunities to learn regardless of the outcomes.[5] These women have the confidence to engage in negotiations, and past success is a primary motivator for being willing to prepare and engage in more negotiations. They put their learning to good use to improve their approach, skills, and resilience for subsequent negotiations. This confidence shows up in the stories women tell themselves: that they have been successful and will continue to be successful.

Workplace as Context

Among the factors that can influence negotiation performance is the context. In this case, we can think of the context as being made up of the culture, policies, and procedures within the workplace. Every organization has its own cultural attributes, some based on the history of the organization, some on the culture of the industry, some on the leadership and management messages, policies, and practices they support and uphold. When there are negative stereotypes about what women should and should not do, especially regarding negotiating behavior, women are disadvantaged before they even arrive at the table. If these messages and behaviors are not consciously curtailed, they tend to be implicitly and explicitly upheld and reinforced.[6]

Expectations of how people will behave, especially as it concerns traditional gender role attributes, and judgment about whether they do what is expected or how their behaviors differ from what is expected, make a difference in how women are received. In these situations, the negotiations are typically conducted with a male style, which is framed to favor men. For example, in mixed gender negotiations, men are often the first to make a move to negotiate and claim value.[7] This is in alignment with what is expected for men according to their traditional gender roles. Making the first move sets the anchor in the negotiation, and whatever comes next is a response to this anchor. Whatever preparation, initiative or goals the female negotiating partner may have had could potentially be sidetracked by this anchor if it was not considered in advance.

Stereotypical negotiating behaviors for women include that they should advocate on behalf of others and not themselves, while at the same time they are told by some of the messaging around them that they need to be more assertive and advocate for themselves.[8] However, on many occasions women are criticized by those who expect them to follow traditional gender behaviors if they do advocate for themselves. This judgment can occur even when men and women use the same negotiating behavior at the bargaining table. A concept called *moral alchemy*[9] helps to explain how such seemingly contradictory judgments are made.

Moral alchemy suggests that there are certain behaviors that are okay for me and people like me to do, but not okay for others in different groups to do. The confusing mixed message goes something like this: I can be as assertive as a man in a negotiation because that is what men do; women need to be more assertive to get what they want; I do not approve of women's assertive behavior because it is outside of the norm, not flattering, and aggressive.

This kind of message is confusing to women. Women are encouraged to behave more assertively, and yet they receive negative reactions when they try something different. As long as the rules about how a negotiation should be done in an organizational context stay the same, this confusion and what some have labeled *backlash* will continue to be present. Here is where there is an opportunity to take a step back and acknowledge that more than a woman's skills at the negotiating table need to be taken into consideration. A more significant difference can be made by changing the rules of the game, and how negotiations are framed.

If the nature of negotiation remains male oriented, women will not do well. They are not able to claim value for themselves if they maintain stereotyped female behavior because they are supposed to advocate for others and not themselves. If they behave according to male standards, as they are sometimes encouraged to do, they can be perceived more harshly than men and are considered aggressive and threatening. It is like being between a rock and a hard place.

These stereotypes of how women should behave have become so ingrained that women adopt them as well and are often not aware that this is what they are doing. In Chapter 1, the ways our personal stories of self are formed and the social stories about how women should negotiate were discussed. These stories are perpetuated so that the stereotypes represented in the social narrative become part of our personal stories. This could lead to self-fulling prophecies that influence how women prepare for and show up at a negotiation and are detrimental to the effectiveness of women's negotiation performance. We see this pattern play out when a negotiator, man or woman, has a woman as the negotiating partner and places lower expectations on the negotiating partner's performance.

Consider the example of negotiating team assignments among team members. If we compare the actions of creating and claiming value as per gendered stereotype, we see that the men on the team might advocate for the work assignments that will allow them to claim value for themselves. If the woman (or women) on the team follows the gender-stereotype behavior or are expected to do so by others, there will be an assumption that they will take the assignments that create value for the team over their own advancement. They will not be expected to claim value first, even if they want to enhance their own performance prospects because that might be considered too aggressive a behavior. Others on the team will not expect the women to challenge the assignments the men have picked, since all assignments need to be completed to advance the team as a whole.

Continuing the example, because the expectations for women to claim value in this case are lower, the male negotiator treats his negotiation targets differently, and the woman negotiator responds to these targets in ways that reinforce the expected behavior. This creates a vicious cycle of having lower expectations and behaving in expected, stereotypical ways, thus reinforcing the negative stereotypes that women do not claim value and do not advocate for themselves, and therefore do not receive as much as they could if they did claim value, is reinforced. To counter this stereotype, women must outperform the lower expectations by seeking more than expected, claiming more value, and walking away with bigger returns.

As this pattern continues, the woman negotiator realizes she is benefitting less than her male counterpart might under these circumstances, and she believes she is a poor negotiator. She develops negative self-talk, an incessant script that plays in her head about how poor a negotiator she is. In turn, she herself sets low expectations for her own negotiating performance. These stereotypes can wreak havoc on a person's self-esteem. The more this negative self-talk continues to loop in her head, the more her performance will decline. This cycle places the blame solely on the woman's performance when, as we have seen, there are other forces at work to create this dynamic.

Organizational Systems and Patterns

In any organizational context there are rules and procedures of how business gets done. These rules and procedures create the system of an organization, and they are not gender neutral. Organizations are social constructions formed to bring people together for the coordinated purpose of providing goods and services. The social practices and gendered stereotypes that are external to the organization are brought in-house and internalized within the organization. So, these external essentialist views of gender-specific behavior are now part of the practice of how the organization is run, and systemic inequities are perpetuated.[10]

To do the business of the organization, a series of negotiations must take place. Sometimes they are formal, and at other times they are informal. Formal negotiations might include vendor contracts, performance reviews, and budget allocations. Informal negotiations are the everyday back and forth about workflow, parsing out work assignments, and figuring out team schedules. Each of these types of negotiations can have slightly different processes and expectations so that the parties within the negotiation have flexibility in how much they stick to the norms. Many of the decision points about how much a negotiator should stick to the usual script or how much they can stray from what is expected depends on the issues being negotiated and the relationship between the negotiators.

The more serious and impactful the outcomes of the negotiation, the more formal the structure needs to be. A decision that seriously impacts the bottom line of a business and determines whether there will be a reduction in the workforce would need a formally structured negotiation, for instance. The way the negotiators behave within that context will be more prescribed because there is so much at stake and risk will need to be assessed.[11] Emotions will be more managed, power relationships and dynamics will be more respected, and there will probably be multiple negotiations on the issues until decisions are made and agreement is reached.[12]

It follows suit that the less serious the issues are, the more flexibility there is for these negotiations to be informal. There is more leeway for the negotiators to take risks, perhaps show emotions and vulnerability, and make daring moves. It is also highly dependent on the nature of the relationship between the negotiators. Informal negotiations are also good for building relationships, clarifying goals and possibilities, and priming a formal negotiation. There is an increased level of comfort and ease between the negotiators by the time they get to the formal negotiation, which is more procedural.

Patterns of Behavior

One of the characteristics of negative stereotyped negotiating behavior is that men are stronger than women at *claiming value*. In a negotiation context, claiming value means that you can assert for yourself and claim what you want.[13] This can be done with or without regard for the benefits to our negotiating partner. In contrast, because some of the stereotyped behavior for women is that they have a stronger concern for others, they may not assert themselves as much, do not claim as much value for themselves, benefit less economically, and end up over time with lower status. Instead, women are more likely to *create value* so that they and others can benefit.[14]

Creating value has its focus on all parties, whereas claiming value is centered on self. Women are known for being more collective in orientation and are better at advocating for others and not only themselves, so it is a natural fit that women create value rather than claim value.

If you think of each negotiation as a one-off deal, then you can isolate it and think, "Oh well, better luck next time." However, there are a couple of things that happen in this scenario that collectively have women in a state that is far worse over the long run. First, in an organizational context, there are incremental advancements that happen over time. For example, if you start at a lower salary than your male counterpart, after several regular performance pay hikes, the gap increases significantly. This imbalance can also happen when it comes to promotions in the workplace. Each promotion has a status improvement attached to it and these status placements also come with access to resources—so higher status and more resources. This, too, creates an incrementally bigger gap that grows exponentially because these seemingly little differences add up to bigger differences.

It is common for a woman to see her male counterpart, who may or may not be as capable as she is, move up the corporate ladder faster than she. She thinks this reflects her own abilities, after which comes the negative self-talk that she is not good enough, not capable enough, and does not deserve more. Skillset aside, there is something dysfunctional in a system that perpetuates these disadvantages. And at the same time, women should learn better negotiating skills because they have the ability to perform and can eliminate that as one reason for slower or less advancement.

One really critical skill that women need to develop is a sense of agency, in that they are in charge of their own destiny, and they are the ones to make things happen for themselves. Many women grew up believing in the fairy tale that Prince Charming would come and rescue them. In following that belief into adulthood, women have given up their power by waiting for others to take care of them, as they were trained to do for others. The only problem with this scenario is that if you wait too long, there is a good possibility that no one will notice, or it will be too little, too late. Too often women in the workplace put their heads down and work expecting that someone will notice and give them the recognition they think they deserve. Thus, it is important to become aware of the attributes associated with each gender so that women can make intentional choices about how they want to be in the world, how much agency they want to apply, and the ways in which they will apply that agency.[15]

Soraya's Story Revisited

In the scenario at the beginning of the chapter, Soraya put her head down and accepted all additional responsibilities given to her. She believed her acceptance of the extra work would be noticed, appreciated, and counted in her favor when it came time for a promotion. However, it was not received the way she had expected. There is a fine line between being a team player, supporting the organization, and maintaining a healthy workload and work-life balance. It was up to Soraya to walk that fine line so she could both be a star contributor and protect herself. Ultimately, she is her best guard.

Soraya will need to assess the situation to determine when and how to speak up so that her impact aligns with her intentions. She will need to weigh the risk vs. reward of any action and decision she makes so that she understands the benefits and the potential repercussions of speaking out against the way things have been done or against the male-oriented paradigm. Of course, women are encouraged to speak up and make their voices heard. This assumes that the playing field is level and that all voices are welcome. There is also an assumption that if a woman does not speak up to challenge the status quo, she supports it. Women then become unknowingly complicit in perpetuating dynamics from which they do not benefit.

The organization's culture, its history, policies, procedures, leadership's messaging, and the stereotypes of women's negotiating performance are all in play and collectively create and perpetuate these dynamics. Women are part of the problem as well because studies show that women also believe that men are better negotiators.[16] Women get in their own way! In addition, when you consider motivations behind wanting to keep the status quo you can see that when people are under threat and when they feel the environment around them that maintains the status quo is under threat they take actions to eliminate said threat.

There are several ways of maintaining the status quo and a gendered workplace. One way is by promoting the idea that men are inherently better negotiators than women. Another way is to "socially punish" women when they are "too" assertive in a negotiation. These tactics can be used overtly or covertly, such as not including women in an email chain or not leaving room at the table, literally. And we all know the unflattering terms that assertive women might be called.

Different Types of Power

A typical way of thinking about power is getting someone to do something you want that the person may not have done on his or her own.[17] Power comes from different sources and, depending on what is valued in a particular context, reinforces what is considered powerful. In an organizational context that is hierarchical, titles are important sources of power. The higher you are in the organization, the more resources you control, and that is a source of power. In a flatter organization that is run with team interactions and teams making the decisions, the team's performance is what makes them more likely to be eligible to make important decisions. You want to be on that successful team.[18]

It also plays out in departments that generate revenues for the company versus departments that, although critical to the organization's success, spend the organization's resources. The departments that are not directly bringing in resources to the bottom line are considered overhead, and the departments that more directly impact the bottom line are the ones with more power. Typically, the sales department and within that department, the strongest performing salespeople wield the most power in an organization.

There are other ways of conceptualizing power. You can think of *dependent power* in which people comply with having a lower rank in an organization and supporting those with power because there is an implicit contract that those in power will take care of those reporting to them.[19] This type of power suits women leaders well, since they are inclined to negotiate better on behalf of others by creating value. Having someone behind you in this way provides for more career development through capacity building and opening doors for networking and advancement.

You can think of the concept of *power with*: the better you do, the better I do, and the better it is for all of us.[20] For example, think about an organization in which different departments work together to provide shared services that support business units. Instead of competing for bigger shares of the budget, the different teams can work together as one. The business unit that interfaces directly with the client appears more effective and efficient when it has stronger support from the shared services teams. The stronger the support team, the better the business unit looks, and all are functioning as one team for the organization. Women who have been known to advocate for others well and who are socially rewarded for doing this well can more readily support this type of power because it matches their style. This type of power is also critical in team performance because, as some have been known to say, "There is no *I* in the word *team*, and therefore, my success is better for the team, as is the team's success better for me."

Women exhibiting *power with* look at negotiation as a collaboration in that the people negotiating ascribe to a higher-level goal—a meta-goal so to speak—so that they are slightly removed from advocating solely for their own self-interests. Of course, within collaboration there is a need for a strong sense of self-advocacy in combination with a strong sense of advocacy for others. It is a delicate balance. It requires a level of trust and information-sharing and does take time in the back and forth.

Collective Intelligence

Taking a collaborative approach to negotiation means you are using cooperative behaviors in the process to get to shared benefits in the outcome.[21] Some of these cooperative behaviors include sharing information and having a strong concern for others, as mentioned previously. This shared concern means there is a greater degree of turn-taking in the negotiation because the intention is to create value for all involved parties. Emphasis is placed on the relationship so that all involved benefit. Whatever happens in any particular negotiation sets the foundation of all future negotiations to build upon, and this sensitivity to the social dynamics is as important as achieving what one sets out to gain as an outcome.

If we refer back to the example of shared services supporting a business unit, there are ways to foster collective intelligence. One way would be sharing information well enough in advance that all units can perform to their highest standard.

Too often, information is withheld, and not necessarily intentionally, until the action is required. When this happens, the business unit is unable to prepare and allocate the necessary resources. Planning and preparing together well in advance of the deliverable's due date allows for all of the contributing units to bring their A-game to the client.

Women have a natural proclivity toward developing and building relational capital. It is a strength that can be turned into an advantage if the framing of negotiation shifts to acknowledge its benefits. This means that a longer-term vision needs to be established because, while there may not be tangible and economic gains in the short-term, the long-term relationship will be an asset in providing a type of stability that comes from deeper and more trusting relationships.

Framing negotiation success to focus on both short- and long-term goals allows for a broader range of practices to be used in the negotiation. This provides opportunities for women to assert more agency in the negotiation and to claim value through creating value for others.[22] Taking a collaborative stance implies that both forms of value are obtained, just through different processes: from traditional, more male-oriented style of engaging in a negotiation to those attributes more closely aligned with a female-oriented style of negotiation.

Another advantage of taking a longer-term perspective on negotiation and building relationships is in what takes place after the negotiation concludes. Once an agreement is reached, it is important to then carry out what was agreed to in the implementation phase. Having a collaborative working relationship with a shared meta-goal to strive toward meeting allows for a more cooperative means of achieving a successful implementation.

If this does not happen and the implementation does not work out well, conflict can arise. The parties would then have to go back to the negotiation table, but with more distrust because of the failed attempts. The starting line of this next negotiation is further back than the original one and a lot more time and focus will need to be placed on reestablishing trust and a working relationship. It may be helpful to think of the process as a series of smaller, small "n" negotiations that happen over time and that lead up to the big "N" negotiation.[23] There will need to be a consistent flow of dialogue and sharing of ideas all throughout the implementation phase to ensure that all voices are heard and any reconsiderations are shared. Unforeseen effects can arise during the implementation phase, and it is just as critical if not more so to continue building trust and a shared goal to address shared interests.

Many types of negotiations occur in an organization. Some of these are formal, and some are the everyday, informal negotiations that we might not even classify as negotiations. They are a part of how we function effectively with others. Gender stereotypes can play a role in how our expectations are set and managed, but too often we perform according to those stereotypes, further embedding them in the organizational culture. Developing awareness of these tendencies is important to better advance individual performance and organizational support for employees.

Reflection Questions

1. In what ways have you claimed value in your negotiations?
2. How do you claim your power in the workplace?
3. In what ways have you modified your mindset or behavior when it comes to your performance in the workplace?

5

Negotiating in Our Families: Families as Systems

As a mother, Audré feels a strong sense of responsibility in raising her children. She talks about how challenged she feels by so many different personalities all living together in the same house. She ends up negotiating much more than she ever expected. She acknowledges it is more difficult for her to negotiate at home than at work because she is so much more emotionally involved, and it was an eye opener for her to realize this. Audré feels it is hard to stay cool and keep perspective when she negotiates with her children about issues they do not agree upon. She ends up leading with her emotions and she knows that it does not help her steer them in the direction she believes is right for them.

Audré becomes overcome with fear about her children's safety, and this emotion overtakes any strategic planning she may have done. And after a long day at work, she is tired and worn down. When she reflects on this issue she sees how, in the middle of engaging with her kids, she fails to take the more level-headed approach. She wants to stay calm and focused when negotiating, stick to the original strategy she prepared, and be in control of her emotional swings.

As we have discussed in earlier chapters, negotiation as a form of communication is grounded or framed in relationships. We negotiate differently when we have a longer-term relationship and deeper mutual knowledge with our negotiating partner than when we do not know each other well. We also take into consideration what our relationship will be like after our negotiation, both during the implementation phase of what was agreed to in the negotiation and after that. There are few, if any, longer-term relationships than the ones we have in our families.

Family Dynamics

There are several ways we can look at family relationships and dynamics. We learn patterns of behavior in our own families that continue to play out, whether we are aware of them or not. There can be unresolved issues that continue to plague us. We may also transfer these issues to other people. If it is too challenging for us to address the issues directly with a particular family member, we may try to address it with another person we place in that role in relation to us. Of course, it may not resolve the issue with the family member, but it might be the best we can do. All of this may operate in our subconscious, so we may not even be aware that this is what we are doing.[1]

Some family members may have good habits that we notice and want to emulate. For example, we may have a family member who is a really good listener. That person sits calmly, focuses on what we are saying, and never rushes us. The person may not offer a solution, and that is okay. We feel heard and acknowledged, and that is the quality we want to carry forward in our communication with others.

Another thing we can learn from observing family dynamics and how they affect our ability to negotiate effectively is that we have preconceived notions of what it means to be in the family role we are in and how we relate to other people. We develop our first emotional ties—for example, making eye contact and being held—in our families, and these sensory inputs will stay with us for a very long time.[2] It will be the foundation of how we deal with emotions in other relationships and for the rest of our lives. This foundation will also shape how we view and understand emotions, our own and others, because of the cultural values and moral judgments we learned from our families. We take this framing into our relationships with others and often make assumptions that others are framing emotions, based on shared values and morals, in the same way we are framing them. However, this is not always the case and can result in conflict that we can look at a little further in the chapter.

Depending on the role you play in your family, you may feel a great deal of responsibility to protect other members of the family, and this will affect your negotiations in more than one way. You may want them to be safe, and you become uncompromising about this factor because you believe that what you are doing is best for them. If your feelings about wanting your children to be happy outweigh your need for them to be safe, this can play out in the negotiation. You may cave in to their demands, over your better judgment, because during the negotiation, your emotional needs for seeing them smile and be happy are stronger. Over time, your desire for them to be safe loses out to your desire for them to be happy, but you still worry about their safety. Your fear for their safety may become overwhelming, causing you to become more emotional, and your emotions may escalate in future negotiations. Thus, your emotional investment in your children's safety may cloud your judgment when negotiating with your children or other family members.

It is important to recognize that our families are webs of relationships. We can take an instrumental approach to negotiating, which basically means we have our self-interests at heart and put those first regardless of the outcomes for others. Alternatively, we may take an altruistic approach, which puts the interests of our family members before our own. The altruistic approach may make us feel good because we are making them feel good, but in the long run we may end up feeling resentful, and that does not serve anyone well. A third alternative is to build on the fact that we are in a web of relationships and can take a more relational view of negotiation in which there are elements of both instrumentalism and altruism because we are combining an approach that considers our own interests, as well as those of our family members.[3]

Family Patterns

Patterns in family systems continue when we are adults, and these learned behaviors impact how we see ourselves in relation to others. These patterns play out in our negotiations. How we prepare, how competent we think we are, how we engage, how we frame the relationship with the other person, all have the potential to be influenced by the relationships we have with our family members.[4] These patterns are also ever present in our internal monologues, in the self-talk that fuels our behavior. They can be helpful or harmful narratives that affect our negotiating abilities.

It is important that we recognize these family relationship

patterns because they will show up in other relationships. For example, we may have specific ideas about what a good mother or father should be, especially as they are the head of the household, and we have expectations that they will protect and provide for us. This may not actually be the lived experience we have with our parents, but it is an idealized profile we have been culturally primed to expect.

In turn, we may transfer those ideals to people in senior positions, who we expect to protect and provide for us. Such an expectation may be met if the senior manager has the responsibility of protecting and providing for her or his subordinates, but in many cases, it is an unfair expectation on our part because that is not the role they actually play. They do not know what we expect of them; thus, our expectations are unreasonable. Imagine how this might show up in our negotiation. We may expect a level of consideration and generosity from the other person, who will not provide it for us; then we will lose on the substance we are negotiating and be disappointed. We might even feel a sense of betrayal. If we have any lingering unresolved abandonment issues from our earlier years, they kick right back up again.

In the previous chapter, we reviewed information on power dynamics. One form of power is dependent power. This dependent power might be in play in a family dynamic and get transferred later in life. We may resist being assertive on certain points because we may not feel a strong need to self-advocate. After all, we are being taken care of by the other party. When we are in a dependent relationship in a family context, the implicit exchange is that we agree to follow because the other party will provide for and protect us. We can see how these preconceived expectations are not realistic and do not bode well for the outcomes of a negotiation and potential future negotiations in a work context, especially with that same negotiating partner.

Dependent power in a relationship shows up in a family

setting when children, who are dependent on their parents, agree to go along with their parents' wishes because they know they are being taken care of by them. Adolescents may agree to clean their rooms, do the dishes, and complete their homework assignment because they know doing so will enhance the chance of being given permission to borrow the family car. If they don't see a potential reward for their cooperative behavior, they may be less likely to comply in a timely manner.

Developing Your Family Story

Our families set the stage for our social narrative formation. It is from our parents that we learn what it means to be in this world and as a member of this family.[5] Siblings and extended family members also help shape our social narratives before we even leave the house to attend school and make friends on the playground. It is the responsibility of our parents and families to socialize us into the world we will inhabit and teach us right from wrong, good from bad, and acceptable or unacceptable behavior.

We also begin our identity development in our families, and sometimes we pick up labels along the way in the form of nicknames or descriptions of how we behave or appear. If we are curious, we might be called the questioner or the doubter, depending on how it is framed. If we do well in school, we may be labeled as the smart one. If we are awkward during our pre-teen and teenage years, labels from that time may continue to follow us. These labels, as discussed in Chapter 3, may be flattering and support our identity development in healthy ways, or be unflattering and harmful so that we develop insecurities.

The feelings about who we are, based on our early years in our families and our identity development, will stay with us and affect us in our adult years unless we recognize and address them. Perhaps when we were younger, we had challenges in school and did not perform well. This feeling of not being smart enough could develop into sensitivities about our competence that show up in a negotiation. We may be more aggressive as we try to prove ourselves, or we may crumble at the slightest hint that we may not know what we are talking about and feel we are in over our heads.

In addition to the messages in our heads, we are also influenced in how we behave. If we like the way our parents treated us, we may want to emulate their behaviors when we have children of our own. If we didn't like the way they treated us, we may promise ourselves that we will act differently. All of these messages in our heads about how to behave, consciously or not, make an impact on how we behave in interactions with our family members.

In Chapter 2, brain wiring was discussed. Our primary wiring is created in our family culture. We can think of each family as having its own cultural characteristics, values, habits, and so on, and all this creates our family culture. This culture is wired into us and carried in our brains. When X happens, we do Y. A child misbehaves and is scolded, punished, or is asked to explain the cause of the misbehavior. Later in life, even if we do not want to behave in a certain way or have a certain type of reaction, we are wired to do so by those formative years.

Even the framing of a particular action as misbehavior sheds a negative light on it. Maybe there was something in the room, a bowl of unguarded candy, that tempted the child to take some. The child's impulse control may not have been developed or sophisticated enough to make a better judgement at that moment, so she ate the candy without seeking permission first. Setting people up for success or failure starts early in life. There will be many temptations along the way, and it is very possible that our first negotiating partner may be ourselves!

Handling Conflict

Another element of family dynamics to consider is the ways our family members handled conflict. Which of them avoided conflict at all costs and tried to either run away from anything resembling a confrontation or smooth over it to make it nice? Neither of these approaches addressed the conflict or the root causes, so chances are high the conflict continued to resurface.[6]

Or perhaps a family member had a confrontational style and everything was fair game to fight over, regardless of the issues, relationship, or outcomes. If this person also had an active temper and was known to blow off steam rather quickly, it may have instilled fear in us, so that we accommodated to smooth over the issues lest this person explode. Maybe we were triggered and joined this person in being confrontational, and then there were two people blowing off steam with no listening or constructive communication.

In any of the above ways of handling conflict, the issues were not resolved, good approaches were not applied, positive outcomes were not reached, and the relationship created more scars. Too often conflicts arise as an unfortunate byproduct of making assumptions that others share the same values and moral judgments as we do. One goal of being in sync with others is to coordinate our actions toward creating shared meanings, and we miss the mark if we do not check the basis of our assumptions.

Because old patterns are engraved in our brains, it is easier to follow the same path we took before even if it does not lead us to where we ideally would like to go. Remember that our families are the place and space where we began our life journey, and some of these patterns are deeply ingrained in our behavior, our identity, and the narratives we carry. Unless we intentionally learn new approaches and skills to manage conflict more effectively, we are doomed to repeat the patterns of the past. Think about the ways in which these tendencies show up in our negotiations.

If we feel uncomfortable—and many are uncomfortable when they feel unprepared or lack confidence—then we will be ready to give in and jump ship at the slightest hint of discomfort. We will need to be aware that our negotiating partner may remind us of a family member and trigger us to fall back into old, unproductive habits. In our preparation, we will need to prepare a strategy and tactics that allow us to respond in the moment, even if it means buying ourselves a slight delay to compose ourselves to carry on again.

Imagine what it takes to change those patterns. First, we need to envision a different outcome. This also means there will need to be a different process. The process includes a different strategy and different tactics, so that we form a different pattern of behaviors and change the nature of the relationship. An interesting dynamic, especially in families, is that once a comfortable pattern has been established, family members might resist the attempts of one member to change the pattern. The grooves of old habits are so deep it will take a concerted effort on multiple parts of the system to make the change, and until a new status quo is reached, it will take extra effort to deal with any resistance.[7]

Creating Your Emotions

Because our emotions use up a lot of physical energy, we will need to budget energy for them. In Chapter 1, we discussed how we make up our social worlds through the narratives we tell and by which we live. The same is true for emotions. A classic definition of emotions says they are predetermined, and all humans are wired to have the same emotions.[8] However, more recently there has been an emphasis on our agency, self-determination, and ability to shape how we understand what is happening to us. The same is true for emotions.

It starts out as our being aware of a bodily sensation we are having and applying a meaning to that sensation. Our past experiences influence how we make meaning of these sensations. If our hearts flutter, and we associate that with the feeling of being scared because in the past our heart fluttered during an event that scared us, then every time our hearts flutter we may associate that sensation with fear. Our brains put together these combinations of a sensory input (heart fluttering) and past experience (fear) to make meaning. We need to understand what is happening to us so that our body can budget the amount of energy we need to keep us alive and healthy. Our body budgets the amount of energy we need by the predictions we make, which are based on our past experiences.[9]

We associate our body budgeting with our relationships; we are relieved when we are with the people we love and burdened when they are not there to offer us relief.[10] Our anticipation of a pleasant or unpleasant event can become a self-fulfilling prophecy. That is, we may make a prediction about the process and outcome of this upcoming negotiation based on a past negotiation we had with a family member that turned out badly, or perhaps our negotiating partner reminds us of someone we knew and negotiated with before. Chances are the negotiation will turn out the way we predicted.

If this is the case, then there may be ways to prime ourselves for success. If we can give ourselves positive feedback for preparing and showing up and encouragement for engaging rather than being solely dependent on the outcome, we have a chance to rewrite the script about who we are as negotiators. This emotional component can be wired into our brains so that future energy budgeting will be made according to this new frame and not that of someone who is easily defeated.

We need to set realistic goals for ourselves and not expect to overcome our biggest challenge overnight. We would be setting ourselves up for failure because it is too big a leap and we would be pressuring ourselves unnecessarily. Instead, we need to think of and create smaller, bite-sized goals that are achievable. We also need to be honest with ourselves and believe in our success and not just give it lip service. If we say our goal is to engage and not shy away, we need to congratulate ourselves for engaging, even if we get nothing we wanted as an outcome of the negotiation. If we commit to not running away or caving in at the first sign of escalated emotions, and instead have a tactic to counter it and use that tactic, we need to congratulate ourselves, even if the tactic failed. The fact that we planned, practiced, and made the effort should count for something.[11]

Changing Our Emotional States

Our experiences are the drivers of our future actions and reactions. A concept called *interoception*, our brain's representation of the sensations in our internal organs, is what allows us to budget the physical energy we will need to foster and manage emotions based on the emotional concepts we already hold from experiences we have had.[12] There is a difference between physical sensations that create our physical reality and the interactions we have with others and our interpretation of those interactions that creates our social reality. We construct and understand our world and our place in it based on our emotional experience of feeling in or out of control. The emotional experience we are having is actually how in control we are, and that leads to our sense of physical, psychological, and emotional safety.[13]

In order to change our emotional responses, we need to take a couple of actions. One is that we need to be more granular in how we perceive and frame our emotions.[14] It is not helpful for us to label an emotional state as one type of emotion. If we feel fear, chances are we are not 100 percent fearful and, in fact, other emotions may co-exist. Maybe we do not feel them as viscerally as fear, so it is easier to look past them and not recognize them when they appear.

Allowing ourselves to look at our emotions with more granularity provides a wider array of emotions for us to construct in any given situation. The adage that if we only have a hammer everything looks like a nail can apply. Looking at our emotions in greater depth is also helpful in constructing a more positive and useful narrative and self-talk. The finer we look at which moments are filled with fear, which have joy, which have bravery allows us to have a finer sense of our emotional experience and increases our emotional intelligence, or our awareness of our own emotions and those of others, and our ability to regulate our emotions. It gives us more to deal with and this fine tuning can enable us to select more appropriate and constructive responses going forward.

Increasing our experience of different emotions develops new emotional concepts in our brains and allows us to have more control over them.[15] Having control over our emotions is something we strive for.[16] If we think of emotions as information, and we are able to more accurately tune in to them, imagine the amount of self-control we will be able to have when we are engaged in a negotiation. We change from blanketing over our emotions to embracing their granularity. It is changing from running away, avoiding, or denying our emotions to being thankful they are there and understanding how useful they can be.

This can be done by being more attuned to the physical sensations we feel when we are in an emotional state. As a next step, instead of immediately going toward categorizing the emotional state with a label, just stay with the physical sensations. This gives us the agency to then determine the label we want to place on the physical sensation and act accordingly. We have a measure of control instead of having a knee-jerk reaction to the physical sensation and then being trapped by the emotional label that may not be helpful to us.

If we are in a situation and we feel our heart flutter, if we are not intentional about categorizing the sensation, then our brain may immediately classify the feeling as fear. Instead, with intention, we can feel the flutter and reclassify the sensation as excitement, maybe anticipation. This can work wonders in energizing us toward our next negotiation.

Our Family Roles

In our families, we learn different roles and the actions associated with them. These are the culturally normed behaviors and attitudes associated with being in that role and can include gender. We learn gender roles from our families, communities, education, and so on. We have been living in a world dominated by a binary view of gender, a view that has been changing over the years to include additional types of gender and the roles and behaviors associated with them. Regardless of how we frame gender, certain behaviors characterize the "good" version of that gender versus those that are outside the norm.

For example, in the US, it has been more permissible for men to express anger than women. Maybe it is because men have been portrayed as protectors and women as nurturers, and anger and nurture don't go together. There has also been a tendency for us to associate emotions expressed by men as being situational, while women's emotions are attributed to their personalities.[17] If we reflect on this, we can see a host of consequences arising from this framing. Men are more stable and predictable because they express emotions in certain situations to ensure a consistent outcome and to control the situation. Women, on the other hand, are unpredictable because their emotions come from their personality and that is the constant regardless of the situation. Women seem to be framed as flawed because they express emotions as part of who they are.

This depiction minimizes just how complex the process and act of expressing an emotion really is. Our brain is processing so many different sensory inputs at once and then trying to allot the amount of energy it needs to predict what will happen next and how to respond. There are multiple feedback loops happening in microseconds, all directed toward keeping us safe. In addition, since we are social beings, our brains are doing all of this work in the context of other people, and their brains are going through the same process; We influence each other's brains by our responses. We are both reacting to and creating new sensory inputs simultaneously, and this has an impact on others around us, which in turn, has an influence on our own brains, and the feedback loop continues.

Dealing with Complexity

I used to be amazed at how complex communication is and marvel that we are able to communicate effectively at all. I can now add brain functions to the mix. It is amazing that our social interactions are at all effective considering just how much is going on in a short amount of time. So much energy is used to keep us safe and maintain our equilibrium. We use the concepts we created about emotions to construct our social realities while simultaneously our social realities continue to influence the creation of our emotional concepts. In Chapter 1, we discussed the interaction of our personal and social narratives, and we can see that this interaction is very much integrated with what is taking place in our brains. Our social situation impacts how our brain is wired, which predicts our behavior, interactions with others, and our social realities. It is a cycle with perpetual feedback loops.

We need to consider how all this plays out in our negotiations. We respond, perhaps unknowingly, to the facial expressions, body language, and spoken words of our negotiating partner. What we interpret and respond to also influences the next move and response and so on, with or without our conscious intentions. However, there is a strong sense of agency involved here when we focus our attention on how we interpret the actions of others, the sensory input we receive, and then how we respond in turn. We feed into the cycles of interactions and our social realities, so it makes sense to be more intentional about what we are doing in those situations so that we achieve better outcomes.

Neurons that fire together wire together in our brains. Being aware of the influences we have from our families, in terms of the roles we play, the values we hold, and the moral judgments we make, we can more intentionally determine how the neurons associate with one another. The conscious framing of effort, regardless of results, is one way of creating a new pairing dynamic that will influence future motivation and a spiraling upwards as we continue to build skills, control our emotional responsiveness, build stronger relationships, and achieve better outcomes.

Audré's Story Revisited

As we explored earlier in the chapter, Audré cares about her children and wants what is best for them on several levels. She wants them to be safe. She does not want to be overprotective and does want to give her children the space to be happy, socialize, and maybe take risks that are part of growing up, such as engaging in physical activities where they could get hurt. She wants them to have friends and enjoy their social life, even if she does not approve of all their friends. She wants them to do well in school and be well-educated and successful in life.

All of these desires for her children shift around in order of priority. Whatever is her greatest concern at the time of the negotiation will be privileged in influencing her stance, tactics, and emotional state during the negotiation. Shifting priorities can happen by gaining access to a new piece of information. Perhaps Audré hears that the child of one of her friends was in a car accident. Now, her own children's safety will take priority, and she might be reluctant to lend them the car. If there is an important event they want to attend, she may decide to drive them herself or find a ride share with another parent.

The diagram below shows the different levels of priority; whatever is at the top influences the mindset and behaviors for all the categories beneath it (Figure 5.1). When safety is a concern, as mentioned above, that shapes all decisions and actions Audré will take regarding her children. When their educational performance is a priority because an important exam is coming up, that will take priority, and she will make decisions with that goal in mind.

The more we know and understand our family origins and the foundational structure and support it gave us, the more we can know the values and moral guidelines instilled in us. We can leave the family stories as they are if they work for us, or we can try to moderate and change them to better suit our needs. Not easy, but possible. At the same time that we are learning more about the ways in which our families influence us, we also become aware of how we are part of social systems. Change must happen within this social context. Our families are our first social system and leave a very big imprint on us both in how we manage ourselves in the world and in how we negotiate.

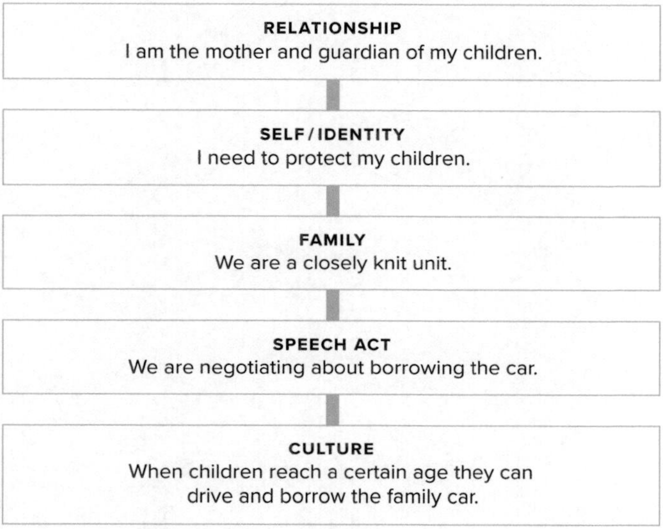
RELATIONSHIP
I am the mother and guardian of my children.
SELF / IDENTITY
I need to protect my children.
FAMILY
We are a closely knit unit.
SPEECH ACT
We are negotiating about borrowing the car.
CULTURE
When children reach a certain age they can drive and borrow the family car.

FIGURE 5.1 Levels of Priority for Audré

When Audré negotiates with her children, she has competing priorities: She wants to keep them safe, but she also wants them to be happy. Her negotiating behavior and outcomes will be dependent on whichever priority is dominant in the current situation. *Based on the Hierarchy Model used with permission by Cronen and Pearce in W. Barnett Pearce, Vernon E. Cronen, and Forrest Conklin from "On What to Look at When Analyzing Communication: A Hierarchical Model of Actor's Meanings."* Communication, *4 (1979): 197; permission conveyed through Copyright Clearance Center, Inc.*

Reflection Questions

1. What are some of the stories you carry with you about who you are that started in your family?
2. In what ways have you modified one or more of these stories to better serve you?
3. How have you generously modified the stories you have of others in your family?

6

Negotiating Personal Friendships and Romantic Relationships

For the last six years, Malu has been in a romantic relationship with Jarvis. She has two children from her previous marriage, and he has three from his. They have decided not to mix the kids together because her children still have a father, and his children have a mother. They are both working professionals and have demanding jobs. Between the time they spend in their careers and being with their respective children, little time is left for the two of them to be alone. Malu is frustrated with this arrangement because she wants to spend more time with Jarvis, Jarvis said he is okay with the amount of time they spend together. She feels this is an ongoing negotiation that she is losing. She wants more time with Jarvis and has tried several approaches to make this happen, but they make a difference only temporarily. Malu questions herself about why this is so important to her. What does spending time with him mean to her?

In framing the components of a negotiation and trying to decide whether to engage, we need to consider the issues and the relationship. A lot of effort is needed in the negotiation process to achieve successful outcomes. That is why it is important to weigh the significance of the issues and substance of what is being negotiated—to make sure it is something we want to continue to advocate for and put in the effort required to make it happen. Then, of course, there is the value of the relationship that determines not only whether it is worth the effort but also how hard we will push to satisfy our needs.

In the previous chapter, where family dynamics were addressed, we noted that the longest relationships we have are with family. We explored the role of emotions and their influence on how we think, feel, and act. Interpersonal relationships, especially those that are close, such as friendships and romantic relationships, are right up there in levels of importance. In some cases, they are more important to us than some of the family ties we have. All of this will influence how we show up for our negotiations.

In all negotiations, there are needs that we seek to satisfy. In a collaborative negotiation, it is important to consider satisfying not only our own needs but also the needs of our negotiating partner. The more important the relationship is to us, both in the present and going forward, the more concerned we will be about making sure the other party walks away from the negotiation feeling satisfied. Negotiations are opportunities to strengthen those relationships.[1]

Now, take a minute to think about how important a certain relationship is to you and how that might affect how firmly you push for what you want. If you think asserting yourself will damage the relationship, you may not push hard. You may accommodate your behavior to your friend's or partner's demands because you do not want to hurt their feelings. These relationships are important to you and having your friend or partner feel satisfied is important, so you may give up some of what you seek in the exchange. This could be a good time to take a minute to make some notes to yourself about what you want, what you are willing to give up, what is negotiable, and what is non-negotiable, to keep you on track for the negotiation.

It is also important to consider in advance whether you are more interested in short-term or long-term gains. When short-term gains are more important, you push harder for benefits gained from the upcoming negotiation. There may be fallout in the relationship because in pushing hard for what you want, you may ignore the gains for the other party, and chances are the other party is losing.

However, if the relationship is important to you, chances are you will be more willing to give up some of your advantages in the short term because you want to maintain a good long-term relationship. In some instances, you may believe that a good relationship will also bring long-term benefits, so winning this particular negotiation is not as critical. This is not always the case. Sometimes the disadvantages do not even themselves out, and in the long-term, the relationship is damaged. There is only so much you will be able to lose without resenting it or eventually pushing back.

The main point here is to frame your advantages and disadvantages from a few perspectives. You want to consider the issues of this particular negotiation and how important they are to you, how connected they are to other aspects of your life, and the longer-term implications of not having them satisfied. Then you also want to look at the quality of the relationship and how central it is to your life. In addition to the issues and relationship, you want to consider the short-term and long-term gains and how they affect satisfying the issues and influencing the relationship.

For many, writing these things down and seeing your list helps in the decision-making process. You can make a chart with four boxes. On the vertical axis are short-term and long-term. On the horizontal axis are issues and relationships. Putting information in each of these boxes will help you see more clearly the weight of the issues compared to the relationship, what can be given up or negotiated, and what is non-negotiable. The time axis can help you visualize what the long-term gains will be and what you can achieve in a short-term frame. It will better prepare you for your negotiation.

Gender Stereotypes at Home

Women are traditionally thought of as nurturers; therefore, it is acceptable for them to advocate on behalf of others when negotiating. Studies have found that when women negotiate on behalf of others, it is more acceptable than when they negotiate for their own interests.[2] It is also thought that women have been culturally prepared to be better at developing longer-term relationships, partly because of their nurturing tendencies and partly because they build on developing networks, such as in a family.

If we consider these to be attributes that are not only placed on women as acceptable behaviors, meaning there will be less pushback, but are actually their strengths, then we can use a nurturing approach as an advantage when negotiating interpersonal relationships. One idea is to explicitly frame the negotiation in terms of mutual benefits. Using the words "we" and "our" makes a difference. As we explored in Chapter 2, words and language use make an imprint on our brains.[3] In turn, the more we use these terms, the deeper the pathways we create, and these lead to specific behavior choices. If your friend or romantic partner continues to hear the words "we" and "our," they begin to accept that there is a mutual gain, their feeling of threat, protectiveness, and competition goes down, and they lean more toward collaboration.

Some of you may be thinking this might sound somewhat manipulative. Yes, if there is no sincerity behind the words and you are using them to be manipulative, the success of this tactic will be short-lived. If you do not mean what you say eventually you will be found out, and any trust that existed in the relationship will be eroded. You will start your next negotiation further back with a new starting line, and you will have that much further to go to be trusted again.

We need more than the sincerity behind the words we say in order to be believed and trusted; the actions taken need to support and carry out what we committed to during the negotiation. This may be challenging if these are new behaviors. It is important to commit to what we can do and commit to trying for the promises made that will be a stretch. A firm commitment can be given with certainty because we know we are capable of fulfilling it. When making a commitment, saying we will try shows that we will put in the effort to make it happen, knowing that there is a possibility it will not work out the way intended because these are new skills and behaviors for us.

One example of this could be in how we make decisions about vacation time. If we start to use the pronouns "we" and "our" to indicate that we view time off from work as shared time, that means we will also collaborate on deciding what to do with this time. We co-create when we jointly engage in making decisions about how to spend the time and where to spend it. When we do this, we give more meaning to the pronouns because our actions follow suit.

The focus in the second commitment is on trying, not the actual commitment. In pairing the neurons that fire together to wire together, there is an opportunity to pair trying on the new behavior with effort, rather than making a 100 percent guarantee that the new behaviors will happen. Our intention to try needs to be communicated and consistently reinforced. It is good to keep revisiting promises and agreements made during a negotiation to remind all involved of what we committed to and to monitor and celebrate the progress made toward meeting those commitments. We should try not to be too hard on ourselves if we have a "slip" in our behavior as long as the intention to make a difference is still alive, well, and being communicated.

Another way of framing our negotiations with friends and romantic partners is thinking of reciprocity: I do this for you, and then you do that for me. This can work when trying to reach balance in a relationship between giving and taking. There are a couple of considerations to consider to ensure successful outcomes and build strong and meaningful relationships. One of the first points to consider is transparency in how much you share of your strategy.

If you decide to behave a certain way and do favors for others expecting favors in return, you need to think about the impression your acts of kindness have on the other person. The person may think these additional behaviors are your normal behaviors and that this is who you are. They may believe you are doing these things expecting nothing in return, so they give nothing in return. If that was your intention, then mission accomplished. However, even if that was your original intention, at some point you might begin to have that old doormat feeling of being taken advantage of, and that cannot feel good. It will build resentment in the relationship dynamic, you will then start counting every act to keep score because it is not a reciprocal relationship.

The way you are giving and not receiving in that instance

is more of an accommodating style, in which the other person benefits and you do not. No one wants to feel like a doormat, and it is not good for maintaining a healthy, balanced relationship. You will need to find a way to assert your needs in the conversation so that your friend knows what to do to keep you satisfied. Healthy interpersonal relationships have a balance, and each relationship needs to find its own balance. It does not have to mean one favor for me and one favor for you. Rather whatever it takes for all involved parties to feel they are giving and receiving fairly. Fairness can be very subjective.

Malu and Jarvis's Story Revisited

Let's look back at the scenario described at the beginning of the chapter, applying these concepts to Malu and Jarvis's story to see how the relationship is working for them. It seems that Jarvis has made a decision about how much time he can afford to spend with Malu, considering all the other obligations he has in his life. Malu understands Jarvis's commitments, and she has commitments as well, but these dynamics are beginning to weigh her down and are eroding her feelings about the relationship. She is frustrated by her inability to get Jarvis to make any changes to his routine. Is the issue really the amount of time they spend together? Another way to phrase this is, "What is really going on here?"

It could be about the time spent together because that is the issue on the table. It could also be about what spending more time together means to Malu. Jarvis has listed all of the reasons why his time is taken elsewhere and that sends a message to Malu that these other items and obligations on his list are more important than she is. She wants to move up the list, and she wants him to be the one to move her name closer to the top. She does not want to force the issue. She wants the change to come from him, yet he does not seem to respond to her subtle and not-so-subtle prompts.

Although at times Malu expresses her desire to spend more time together, she also feels guilty and selfish pressuring Jarvis. It is a no-win situation for Malu that is keeping her trapped in the dynamic of feeling unhappy in the relationship. There are some choice points Malu needs to make going forward so that she can engage in a more personally gratifying and meaningful relationship. One way is for Malu to be honest with herself and admit that she wants more attention from Jarvis and that she wants to be more important to him.

She may be important to him, but he cannot show it in the way she wants. Malu needs to think about other ways Jarvis can show how important she is that he is able to do. In negotiation terminology, we may call this taking a position. In this case, Malu makes the demand of wanting more time with Jarvis, and Jarvis says he cannot give her more time. This is not a win-win situation if they stay at the positional level of time/no time. Instead, they need to dig down deeper to see what is really driving these positions, going to the underlying level of needs fueling these positions. What is really going on here that is causing both of them to take these stances?

Malu may have needs that include wanting more attention, recognition, acknowledgement, love, and intimacy that can be satisfied in several ways, professionally and personally, yet she sticks to the position of more time with Jarvis. Jarvis may have the needs of wanting more autonomy, recognition, and love that he can get from his career and Malu, but he frames that as spending more time with his children, resulting in less time with Malu. If they focus on satisfying their needs and moving away from their current positions, they have a wider playing field with more options from which to choose. It is shifting the focus from time being the only way to satisfy their needs to other ways of showing how important they are to one another.

At the same time, Malu needs to accept that there are different ways to have her needs satisfied. Having her needs met does not mean settling for a lesser substitution or she will not find it satisfactory. Malu and Jarvis will need to have a conversation about their relational dynamics and having their underlying needs met. An important aspect here that should not be diminished is that Malu needs to give voice to her concerns and let Jarvis know how she feels. He may think he is doing all he can and not realize Malu is harboring resentment or why. He may just feel the pressure from Malu's demands of more time, not understanding what is driving her to push on something he feels he cannot give.

Once Malu has identified what is meaningful to her and she has thought about the different ways she can see her commitment, she also needs to acknowledge that Jarvis may not be able to give her what she needs. Malu will need to accept that this is just the way he is, that her needs are important, and she will need to weigh whether being in an unsatisfying relationship is better than not being in a relationship at all. She will also need to believe in her own sense of self to make a choice that may result in taking that leap out of the relationship and be open to finding another that is more satisfying for her, or the risk that it may not happen at all.

Even the thought of framing these relationship choices can leave Malu feeling vulnerable.[4] She is, admittedly, taking a great risk, and it may not feel good. However, the current state of the relationship is also not feeling very good. It is a matter of choosing which discomfort she will take. The discomfort of advocating for herself and negotiating on her own behalf for what she wants in the relationship will at least give her the chance to find more positive outcomes. She can use a combination of pronouns in her negotiation, starting with "we" and "our," to focus on the mutual benefits in their relationship. Then, at some point, she will need to switch to "I" so she can advocate for what she wants.

For Malu, going through the process of weighing options and realizing that she can have a stronger sense of agency to advocate for herself is empowering. It does not mean she will get what she thinks she wants or deserves, but it does mean she can take care of her needs and protect herself. It might put her in a position where she feels vulnerable but not helpless. She is putting herself in this situation because she has thought through the situation, and she knows that she can choose other options. It is a wonderfully freeing place to be knowing that she does not have to settle for relationships that are not working well for her. Malu needs to consider her BATNA of staying or leaving the relationship. BATNA refers to Best Alternative to a Negotiated Agreement, and Malu needs to see her other options and how they compare to staying in the relationship.[5]

Remember that there are short-term and long-term aspects for Malu in making these choices. In the short-term, the choices may not feel good because she may feel that she is losing something meaningful. Malu needs to ask herself whether these choices are worth it or not. If the current situation is tolerable and even more than that, bringing her joy, then she should make the choice to stay. However, if it is not and the negative aspects are more than the positive and it is bringing her down, Malu should make the choice to go.

The act of making the choice is what is empowering. Of course, with choosing comes responsibility; Malu needs to accept that she is responsible for the choices she makes. Not everyone wants to handle this responsibility, and that is something to acknowledge for herself too. Then I would ask Malu to consider whether she would rather be making the choices for herself or letting others do it for her. Either way, she is making a choice of asserting her sense of agency or choosing to let Jarvis make the decisions.

For Me Versus for Us

Personal and intimate relationships have a longer shelf life than some of our professional relationships and our informal everyday relationships with vendors. Therefore, there is a strong incentive to want to make them successful for us and for the person with whom we are negotiating. As we have discussed framing negotiations earlier in this chapter, both we and our negotiating partners have interests and needs. Some of these interests and needs may overlap or be complementary. Sometimes they seem to be in opposition to one another, and while that could be the case, it may also be the case that the focus is on the positional stance, not necessarily the underlying needs.

When we make a demand, even softly so that it may not seem like a demand, we are staking a claim for something we want. Our demand, or position, is but one way to fulfill that need, although it may not seem that way at the moment. It may seem that we are being reasonable, and this is what we want. If our friend, partner, or spouse wants something that appears to be in opposition, then we are at a standstill because we are stuck at the positional level. We cannot go and stop at the same time, nor stand and sit. We need to ask ourselves what is really going on so that we can dig deeper and see what we and the other person really need. This deeper dig can open so many more possibilities when we are at the needs level because we get to be more creative at finding ways to satisfy those needs.

When we are more focused on the outcomes of the negotiation rather than the relationships and the negotiation is a means to an end, think about the effect it has on these meaningful, long-term relationships. Nobody likes losing, especially on a repeated basis, and they will likely become further entrenched as time goes on. At the same time, we do not always want to cater to the needs of others, even if it does satisfy feelings of altruism, since that means we are consistently losing.

It is important to take a relational approach to negotiation so that we focus on the outcomes and how they are achieved while taking care of the relationship.[6] Doing so allows us to feel satisfied because we have negotiated to get what we need, and we have built social capital along the way in supporting our friend, partner, spouse, in getting what they need. This orientation begins with the preparation stage when we are framing the negotiation, and carries through goal-setting, engaging in the negotiation, coming to an agreement, and implementing the agreed-to actions to reconfirm our commitment.

We have said that women are known for their ability to nurture and care for others, an attribute that can be considered both a strength and a hindrance. The ability to nurture allows for attachments to be formed, and as social beings we need these kinds of connections. Let's take a deeper look at what lies behind developing social relationships and attachments and how it might play to our advantages when negotiating.

Attachment and Social Interactions

Another attribute that influences our healthy emotional and cognitive development is how we develop attachments to others. Our attachment starts in infancy, and healthy development leads towards knowing when to avoid or engage with others.[7] When we are in situations that feel safe, we want more closeness to those with whom we feel safe. Likewise, when we are in situations that feel threatening, we want to avoid those people who feel threatening. These nurturing tendencies that lead to developing attachments have been associated with women as mothers. Research in recent years has shown that fathers can also foster healthy attachment in their young.

Most of us have had the experience of having a strong first impression of a person; we either feel comfortable with them or we don't, and we need to pay attention to these feelings and explore them. We also develop a sense of connecting with others to rely on them for emotional support when we need them to reduce our levels of stress. Otherwise, we must manage everything on our own. We also have an inherent belief based on our past experiences that being with others brings benefits and that these relationships are rewarding. Oxytocin is released into our systems. Oxytocin is a feel-good chemical that reinforces the rewarding nature we associate with these types of social interactions.[8]

When we do not develop a healthy attachment toward others, our emotional regulation abilities are hampered, our responses are not always helpful to us, and we do not associate being with others as rewarding. We are not sure whom to trust, and even our own senses may betray us about who feels safe and when there is a supposed threat. We may not have good judgment about how much and with whom we should engage, and we may engage more than we should with those we should avoid. Our reactions to keep ourselves safe may not kick in when they should. We also do not have people we can rely on to collaborate and support us to reduce our stress levels. Remember, we are social beings, and while we do develop the ability to manage on our own, we also relish the support of others. Without this support, we must learn to address these threats on our own.

In some instances, continuing to support ourselves may work out well because we develop strategies and tactics to manage well independently. In other situations, we may not develop useful and beneficial strategies and then we must deal with the additional stress, which over time can have ill effects on our health. We may develop self-soothing strategies that could take their toll on us later in life. Our brains, in predicting what we will encounter on any given day, prepare us by budgeting the amount of energy we will need to maintain our lives.[9] If the budgeting does not account for prolonged periods of stress, we use up more energy than is available. We over-tax certain parts of our brains by relying on them more than we have budgeted, and the result is a negative impact on our health.

Our bodies and brains are not prepared to manage well during long periods of stress. We produce the chemical corticosterone in stressful situations, and it affects our immune system.[10] Think back to times when you felt stressed and what happened to your brain and body functions. You were not operating at your optimal capacity, and perhaps your judgment also became impaired. This cannot bode well for your relationships and certainly will not prepare you to be your best in a negotiation. It's a good idea to make notes about the high stress times in your life and what happened to you physically, mentally, and emotionally. Then look for patterns in the symptoms you experienced at these stressful times. You want to develop strategies for lowering stress so that you can function as your best self.

The challenge here is that while we need to develop our own strategies for how to be safe and when to form healthy attachments, we also need to do this in sync with others. Because we are social beings, we need the healthy interactions and support we give and get from being with others.[11] When we are emotionally and cognitively secure, we are able to use strategies of self-regulation when necessary as we do our own threat assessment in our environment.[12] We are also able to co-regulate with others as necessary. Being able to switch as appropriate is an advanced stage of emotional regulation. We can call on constructive strategies because we can continually assess and reassess threats and negative thoughts to make sure they are real and that our assessment is reliable.

Think about how this may show up in our negotiations. We may be in situations where we trust the person we are negotiating with, so there is a stronger inclination to engage rather than avoid. However, if we do not trust them or our own judgment, our sense of how much to engage or avoid may be out of whack, and our negotiations will suffer as a result. We will not employ the most beneficial strategies and tactics because we are under duress from the stress of not being able to trust. Reflecting on the level of trust we have in these situations can help guide us in the decisions we make.

Interacting with Others

Another fascinating development from neurosciences is that, in addition to what goes on inside our own brains, we are influenced by the brain activity of those around us.[13] This may sound like something from a sci-fi flick—someone is exerting brain control over us. If our negotiation outcomes do not work out well, we can always say, "He made me do it." However, research shows that we are influenced by what is happening in the brains of others.[14]

This concept is called bio-behavioral synchrony,[15] and it occurs because we are social beings, and our social interactions relate to our survival. It is also referred to as interpersonal attunement[16] –that feeling of being in sync with someone else and feeling especially attuned to them. Synchrony is especially relevant in our interpersonal negotiations. If we hold the other person's interests in serious consideration and we want them to be fulfilled, we can communicate that on an unconscious level, brain to brain, in addition to all of the overt comments and actions we take.

Our unconscious communication will signal to our negotiating partners that we are sincere in what we are saying because we are communicating that on multiple levels. At the same time, because we might be at a disadvantage of getting what we need from the negotiation, we also need to remain vigilant on that front. Another way to think about this is not that it is selfish or self-serving, but that both sides benefit from outcomes when we both are satisfied. The more cooperative we are, the more our inter-brain coherence increases, further reinforcing the sincerity between us and the tendencies to gain trust and achieve positive outcomes.

While our first personal relationships are with our families, we choose many other relationships at different stages of our lives. We have an emotional investment in them, and they are meaningful to us. There are several situations that will arise in the course of these relationships that will require us to negotiate for what we need. Sometimes our original attraction to a relationship is no longer meaningful and we will need to reassess how important the relationship is and how much effort we want to apply to prolong it. As long as our relationships are important and meaningful, applying constructive negotiation skills will continue to make sense and will add to the enjoyment and benefits of the relationships.

Reflection Questions

1. How have you become more conscious of what is important to you in your personal relationships?
2. In what ways have you developed a better BATNA?
3. What strategies and tactics have you used to negotiate for what you want?

7

Negotiating Outside of Work and Family

Crystal wanted to build her brand recognition and expand her business as an executive coach. As a faculty member at a prestigious university, she was sought after by others who wanted to engage her as a coach for their professional development. Crystal was comfortable reciprocating offers as one professional to another when they made sense, such as sharing resources, introducing colleagues, and referring clients. She also was willing to support others even without reciprocation because in her mind that is what good colleagues and mentors do for one another.

However, it seemed that some used the pretense of a coaching conversation as a way to advance their own agendas, with no intention of actually being coached. They may have wanted an introduction to another colleague familiar to Crystal, or perhaps they wanted to learn about her approach, something she would have appreciated their stating up front rather than pretending to come to her for coaching.

Crystal felt uncomfortable with those conversations that seemed self-serving and coerced. In these situations, she often felt at a loss about how to make the encounter more of a give-and-take so that it did not leave a bad taste in her mouth. Crystal questioned the intentions of these people in reaching out in the first place and wondered if people met with her because they genuinely appreciated what she had to offer or if they were only interested in using her for their own advancement.

When we interact with strangers or people with whom we do not have a strong relationship, we initially place less emphasis on the relationship and more on the substance and outcome of the interaction. We don't yet have an established relationship, so it could be a more transactional encounter at first. For example, if we connect our negotiation performance with a strong sense of self, we will be more sensitive to how well we do in any of these encounters. Because they are impersonal—we may never see the person again—these types of negotiations have less of a personal impact on us. However, if we connect our performance in these everyday negotiations directly to our self-narrative, identity, and overall sense of who we are and whether we can assert and take care of ourselves and negotiate well, then the process and outcomes of these negotiations will be important to us.[1]

What We Can Learn from Everyday Negotiations

If the stories about ourselves are filled with narratives of not being good enough, not being competent, we may even feel defeated by our local dry cleaners when they do not give us the best price for cleaning our clothes. This encounter will reinforce our feelings of failure because even our dry cleaner is more competent than we are in negotiating. (This is not to say anything disparaging about dry cleaners; remember that they negotiate every day all day, so their experience level is high regardless of their attitude and skills.)

We may also carry a story about what is and is not expected of us as women in this world, especially when it comes to negotiations. Cultures, societies, and our social worlds have gender codes about what women should do, where they have strengths, and spaces and places they should not venture.[2] If we do venture out, there can be backlash and other unpleasant outcomes. Our gendered perspective is a lens on how we see the world around us[3] and that in turn shapes our behavior and the ways we continue to shape our social worlds. We have choices that lead us to either follow prescribed gender profiles or step outside of those boundaries, intentionally or unintentionally.

Let's reframe how we look at these types of encounters. We can use these everyday negotiations as opportunities to try out new skills we are learning and want to practice. These are low-stake negotiations; if our tactics do not work, no big deal. We tried them, saw the results, and will modify accordingly next time because there *will be* a next time. We need to continue practicing, developing our negotiating muscle so that every time we enter into a negotiation this muscle memory will be triggered and we will be at a better starting point.

We can be relaxed about these minor negotiations (small "n" because we are not negotiating major issues) because they are not tied to our identity and sense of self. Once they are connected to the ongoing feedback loop of the script in our head of who we are, they get spun into the rest of our narrative. Of course, when the script is positive, and we are able to put these everyday negotiations into perspective, they can strengthen our sense of self of who we are as negotiators. We continue to hone our skills and celebrate ourselves for the small gains we make. Even if sometimes it feels like we are taking two steps forward and one step back, there is still a forward trajectory.

On the other hand, if the script in our head saying we are not good enough continues to loop, it reinforces those negative feelings of self. The negative loop will keep us mired in the trap of feeling less than. At these times, it is good to take a step back and ask ourselves how important these negotiations and people are in our lives, especially compared to those who are really important and have more meaningful roles. Everyone cannot have the same level of importance, so it is a useful exercise to start to differentiate them.

All of the people we interact with continue to influence the social narrative of our lives. This in turn influences our personal narrative. As we discussed in Chapter 1, our narratives are fluid, and all our interactions can influence them. We can have agency and decide just how much of an impact we will let them have on us. If we want to change the level of influence because we do not like the direction the story formation is taking, we can develop a counter-narrative.

These negotiations that have lesser importance are an excellent training ground for trying out new skills. They can support us in developing our skills while also serving as good material for changing our narrative about who we are as negotiators. The risks are low, and the obstacles getting in the way of our performance are small. Of course, we may still be judged on how well we do, but since we are putting these negotiations into context, the judgments are feedback that we can keep or discard. We have control over that part. It is also good to keep in mind that feedback is as much about the person that is giving it as it is about the receiver. It lets us know what that person pays attention to, but we can decide how to use that information.

Deception, Manipulation, or Telling the Truth

In our negotiation preparation and during the process of the actual negotiation, we may wonder how truthful we should be with the other person. We have a choice about how much we should reveal to the other side, and when trust is an issue, we should be cautious about how much we reveal. In a cooperative negotiation, when both sides are sincerely interested in the outcomes for the other party as well as their own outcomes, there is usually more open communication.

Being open does not mean blurting out everything we know in the first few minutes. It is important to decide what to share in the initial phases and what to withhold until later. Then, of course, there is information that is not to be shared at all because it does not enhance our position in the negotiation and, in fact, may seriously weaken our negotiating position.

An example of this could be when we do not have a strong BATNA, a strong alternative outcome to this particular negotiation. We really need this negotiation to go well because it is our best and maybe only option. Information is power. The more we know, the stronger the position. The same is true, of course, for the other side. In addition, when negotiating, we expect that there is something being withheld and during the negotiation we try to uncover this missing—or perceived to be missing—information. The same is true for our negotiating partner.

If we reveal all of our information too early in the negotiation, and we claim we have nothing left to share, our negotiating partner may not believe us and therefore begin to mistrust us, the opposite of what we wanted. Even so, we do not want to reveal that we do not have a strong BATNA because that information will strengthen the other party's position, and it will not bode well for us.

When we negotiate with people we know well, we are able to read them better because their way of thinking and their mannerisms are familiar. We have a better sense of when they are being honest and when they are not. Call it our sixth sense, if you will, because different signals go off in our heads that may make us question their sincerity. Likewise, they are able to read us more effectively. In the previous chapter, we talked about how our brains communicate with one another in social settings even if we are not conscious of this communication. Thus, something is happening at the brain-to-brain level that raises potential suspicions in us about how truthful they are being.

When we negotiate with strangers or people we do not know well, we still have an interbrain communication happening in the social context of our interaction. We may get a sixth sense about whether we can believe the other person or not. Fascinating studies have been done looking at what happens in our brains when we are telling the truth or deceiving others. Even initiating the intention of potentially deceiving others makes a difference in our brains.

When we negotiate, we use the front parts of our brain, which is where most of our cognitive functioning takes place. The advancement of MRI imaging has allowed brain researchers to see more of what happens in the brain during certain activities. Researchers have done studies showing that we use more cognitive processes when we deceive others than when we tell the truth.[4] These processes include making decisions about what we will expose versus what we will hide. For example, we need to inhibit our own "error detection mechanisms" when we are not telling the truth so that it doesn't stop us from not telling the truth! Needless to say, we use up a lot more energy to maintain the deception than to tell the truth.

In the case that there is an inclination not to trust or believe others, even when they come forth with the truth, we can feel deceived. This has been labeled as "sophisticated deception" because it is more difficult to pull off than regular, everyday deception.[5] Deceiving others with false statements is considered to be manipulation. Sometimes people wonder if telling part of the truth is still being truthful or if it is lying. Rest assured that it is still considered a form of manipulation because when you are intentionally withholding information, it is a manipulation with the intent to deceive. Your brain activity reveals similar usage when you're manipulating the truth and when you are being sophisticatedly deceptive.[6]

Crystal's Story Revisited

In thinking back to the scenario described at the beginning of the chapter, it seems that Crystal may have been feeling manipulated. The request for coaching may not have matched the actual ask (although not framed as an actual ask) of looking for a favor, and this inconsistency caused Crystal to suspect that this was the other person's intention all along. Crystal knows that if the person had made the real request up front, she probably still would have engaged with the person to some degree. However, the deception, which could be called a "bait and switch," did not sit well with Crystal.

This experience also caused Crystal to question why she wants to feel connected and be supportive of a stranger. Part of it is that she realizes she is subject to the influence of the social narrative around her of what good women do and what good colleagues do to support others. She puts herself second in these situations and is much more willing to accommodate others and help them on their professional journey. Crystal could be suffering from what research has labeled the likability factor, in which women seek to be liked and do not want to be perceived as self-serving, even if it is not at the expense of others.[7] All of these thoughts in Crystal's head will influence how she negotiates with these individuals and will then influence the outcomes of their working relationship.

Taking Risks

We are more inclined to take risks when stakes are low because we do not have much to lose. These stakes can include the issues we are negotiating, the outcomes we are seeking, and the importance of the relationship. If the issues are critical to us and we do not have much wiggle room in achieving the outcomes we seek, and if the other person is an important part of our lives, these would be considered high-stakes situations, and we will have more on the line to lose. Therefore, that would probably impact the level of risk we are willing to take, and we will be more risk-averse, meaning conservative in what we ask for and in our performance. However, if it is all or nothing, we may take more risks because we do not want to lose it all.

Making decisions about whether to take risks and the act of risk-taking itself was thought of as being emotionally engaging. After all, there are important issues, outcomes, and relationships at stake. There are different types in this decision-making process, which Kahneman refers to as type 1 and type 2 decisions.[8] Type 1 decisions are quicker, more reactive, more impulsive, and more emotional. Type 2 decisions, on the other hand, are made more slowly, involve more information, are not impulsive, and use more cognitive brain processes. They may seem to be more rational than type 1 decisions.[9]

Recent studies[10] have shown that thinking of decision-making about risks as either emotional or rational creates a false dichotomy. Instead, researchers propose that we think of how much of our brains or cognitive processes are involved in the decision-making process. Using MRI scanning of the brain during decision-making processes, researchers have found that there is lower cognitive engagement when making type 1 decisions that are quicker and more habitual, whereas type 2 decisions that take longer and are more thoughtful use more cognitive abilities.

The type of risk affects our risk-taking orientation. When something is perceived as low risk, we are probably framing it as a type 1 problem to solve. Framing a situation as a type 2 situation, with higher stakes and more to lose, may cause us to be more risk-averse, slowing down the decision-making process.

Likewise, if we have something to lose at stake, we are less constrained to take risks. We want to do whatever we can to avoid loss. On the other hand, when we see there is something to gain, we are more risk-averse because we do not want to jeopardize the potential gains at stake. This is one of the reasons the way we frame a negotiation, especially when it comes to risk and reward, has a direct effect on how we engage in it. More specifically, the risk level of what is at stake in the negotiation influences the strategy we select, the behavior and tactics we use, our level of confidence to carry out the strategy, and our emotional state.

We need information to make better decisions and to perform more accurate risk assessments. When we are in situations that are new to us with people who are also new to us, this information is harder to obtain. We need to trust our gut instincts because our brains communicate information to us of which we may not be consciously aware. It is good to pay attention to these signals as cues for further inquiry to understand why we are having these sensations in the first place.

Reflection Questions

1. What skills have you practiced in your everyday negotiation? How can you use everyday negotiations to improve your skills?
2. How do you become aware that someone is potentially manipulating you?
3. How do you reward yourself for every success, no matter how minor?

8

Negotiating Compromising Situations

There was no getting around the fact that whenever Vanesa had to meet with the head of sales, she cringed. There was something about his mannerisms and the way he looked at her that seemed sleazy. He didn't do or say anything overt, but there was something about him that made her uncomfortable. She always tried to meet him with others around to avoid what might turn into an unpleasant situation. By avoiding him, however, she also missed opportunities to demonstrate her value to the firm, something that could be costing her better client engagements. He does have a big influence in the firm and could be valuable to her career. She wondered if he knew she was avoiding him.

We may be in situations that make us feel uncomfortable, and we need to recognize this discomfort. The need to feel safe and secure is basic, and our primal detectors may sound off when we feel threatened emotionally, psychologically, physically, or morally. It is good to acknowledge these physical sensations and feelings and question what is causing them. It can be what some refer to as our "spidey sense," or sixth sense. We have these sensing mechanisms for a reason: our overall safety.

We can consider a range of situations that are uncomfortable and threatening and have a wide range of consequences, depending on whether we take action and which action we take. This statement is based on the premise that there is still time to negotiate our way out of a situation. Of course, if there is any imminent danger, we should immediately leave if we can and take our actions away from the danger. There may be a delicate balance between wanting to nip something in the bud so that it does not escalate and making sure that what we suspect is actually taking place.

Because these are difficult situations, we may try to avoid them if we can, and in some instances that is the best strategy. However, there are times when we are suddenly in the middle of a difficult situation that we did not anticipate, but we still have time to negotiate our way out of it. Taking an action of some sort is a way of taking control over our lives and showing agency. Regardless of the outcomes or how well we perform our negotiation tactics, the fact that we made a choice and took responsibility is what we should focus on.

Whether we deal with the situation on our own or let someone else take the lead, the constants are that we are uncomfortable and the situation is difficult. The difference is whether we exert agency, make a decision, take action, and boost our self-esteem because we took action or do nothing and let something happen us. This use of our agency fuels the positive and constructive narrative in our heads. There is also a higher chance of a better outcome when we are in the driver's seat rather than being a passenger and having the situation come to a conclusion we do not want.

There are other negotiations we can have that do not involve the person directly. We can ask decision-makers to change our situation, especially in the workplace. This can be a tricky conversation if we are still unsure that what we are sensing or experiencing is real. We may feel that we do not have enough specifics about the actions a person has taken against us.

It can also be challenging if the person we are raising concerns about is a star performer and a favorite in the company. This is especially true if this star performer brings in revenue that feeds the bottom line. At the end of the day, if we are feeling compromised, we have to make choices. It is a matter of risk and reward and, unfortunately for several women in the workplace, the risks are far greater than the rewards. Some of this has changed with the #MeToo movement, which has given more women the courage to raise these concerns and for organizations to take them seriously because of potential legal and image consequences.[1]

I want to note here that it is not just women who may feel uncomfortable with unsolicited advances from others that are not only unwanted but also threatening. Chances are that if you are sensing these unpleasant vibes from a person or if he has made more overt advances, others have also experienced the same or similar from this person.[2]

Another note is that I use the pronoun *he* because historically men have held the power in organizations and have been accused of creating more compromising situations in the workplace, but the problem is not limited to one gender. It is simpler when writing to limit to one pronoun and this book is focused on women, although the practices recommended are applicable to everyone.

Disgust as an Emotional Response

There has been some interesting research about disgust. I initially did not think it was a category all its own, but it seems that there are scholars who specifically study disgust. What caught my eye in reading some of this research and how it is applicable to this chapter is that disgust is an emotion that can lead to behaviors that regulate our exposure to harm.[3] When we are in a situation that gives us a creepy feeling and causes us to feel emotions we could classify as disgust, our brains are trying to keep us safe.

When our brains are trying to keep us safe, they are measuring the amount of risk exposure we have. Research has shown that there are sex differences in levels of tolerance for risk. Men have more tolerance for risk and are more accepting of risks when there are potential benefits attached.[4] Of course, this is a blanket statement, and there are individual dispositional factors to consider because not all men and women will behave the same. In addition, there are several situational factors that influence the decision-making process, such as types of risk, levels of risk, and benefits attached.

Some of the research on disgust focuses on *moral disgust*, which is the sense that someone has broken social norms and is not abiding by widely accepted moral codes. Moral disgust protects us from direct harm and from social stigma. We move away because affiliation with the person who is causing moral disgust is dangerous; our reputations can be tarnished based on the people with whom we associate. We want to employ strategies that will keep us safe, but it is important to consider our social standing too. Sometimes just being associated with people who have questionable moral characters tarnishes our own standing.

One challenge in all these avoidance strategies is that lack of interaction leads to a lack of familiarity, which could also work against us in terms of advancing our careers. There are many times in organizations when we need to work with people we may not like or who make us feel uncomfortable. We can also leave the organization, but there is no guarantee we will not encounter something similar in our next workplace.

Vanesa's Story Revisited

In the case of Vanesa's story, her avoidance of the head of sales also meant that he did not fully see Vanesa's value as a member of the sales team. He did not get to know her worth and, therefore, may not have considered her for prize assignments and promotions. Part of getting ahead in an organization is being known and being at the right place at the right time, which we cannot do if we are not present.

The first priority, of course, is our safety. The actions we should take are all about making us safe and secure. We have a couple of choice points at this stage. We should always have a comment to say or a move to make as an immediate response to get us out of the potentially compromising situation. This is to protect us from any immediate harm or escalation of the situation. It is worth noting here that this is a specific situation in which Vanesa needs to make a decision concerning how to feel safe. In other situations when we feel uncertain and unsafe, we need to explore the sources of this discomfort. If there is an imminent threat, we need to remove ourselves and ponder the source at a distance in a safer place.

Making Choices

If we are dealing with someone who makes us feel uncomfortable, we can let the person know directly that we do not appreciate his comments and that we are all about business and not interested in anything else. This level of directness can feel risky, because if we are not sure of his intentions in the first place, we do not want to appear foolish. However, it is also us taking charge of our safety and letting him know that even if he did not have these intentions, he is still doing something to project that he does. It is good feedback for him.

Another action we can take is not to put ourselves into situations where we are alone with him. We need a third person who will always be a buffer between the two of us and a witness to the dynamics. We can also speak to someone else, a neutral person or a person who handles these types of situations and can advise on what to do. And then, of course, we can always speak to someone in authority to raise these issues.

There can be backlash from taking overt actions. In some cases, the person against whom these accusations are made will retaliate. In other situations, we can be labeled as a troublemaker or someone who is not well or who is encouraging these situations to occur. We need to be strong in our own conviction that we are protecting ourselves.

People will react in all sorts of ways. Some of their reactions may reflect their own internal guilt about not protecting us, having seen the other person's unacceptable behavior.

Sometimes they know about the behavior and choose to look past it because the person is still valuable in the organization or is a family member. At the end of the day, taking action to protect ourselves is key, and this is the story that needs to be part of our overall narrative. Of course, there may be consequences to our career, and we may need to leave our workplace for an environment in which we feel safer. If it is a friend or family member we are raising concerns about, it may strain some of the surrounding relationships as well.

All of these considerations need to be accounted for as we make our decisions and weigh the risk and reward factors. We have our own levels of tolerance about what we are willing to put up with and where there is a very firm line that we will not cross. It is good to reflect on our boundaries so that we know in advance and are prepared for a difficult encounter. The more prepared we are, the more we can respond automatically in the situation and not let our actions be distracted by emotions that may overtake us at the moment.

In the next section, we will explore different ways in which we can be better prepared for negotiations, formal and informal.

Reflection Questions

1. What signals alert you that a situation is potentially compromising?
2. What strategies and tactics do you use to keep yourself safe?
3. Who can you call on for guidance and support in these situations?

PART 3

NAVIGATING THE FUTURE

9

Lessons to Take with You: Negotiation Preparation

This chapter is the first of three that put together a blueprint for how you might engage in your future negotiations. It takes some of the principles, practices, and information covered in this book and also draws on other best practices in the field. The chapters are divided according to the phases of a negotiation: preparation, process, and post-negotiation. Then, within each of the three chapters, there will be sub-sections, or mini episodes, leading to the complete negotiation.

Preparing for Your Negotiation

There are several aspects of a negotiation to consider in advance. The more prepared you are, the better able you will be to remain in control of yourself and the negotiation, and the less chance you will be stalled, stymied, or just plain overwhelmed. Of course, there are always possibilities that new information will come to you in a negotiation that you had not anticipated; however, the process of preparing also gives you the confidence you need to tackle any situation effectively. The more you plan for several possible scenarios, the more agile you will be in the negotiation and the more able you will be to pivot and continue on effectively.

Framing

The first step in preparing for a negotiation is to adjust your mindset so you can be your most focused, centered, positive, and strong self. Your self-talk needs to be about success to boost your morale and confidence. Framing is therefore an important part of the pre-preparation phase of any negotiation because it sets you up from the get-go for success.[1] As discussed in the introduction of the book, you may be one of those women who is uncomfortable about negotiation, a feeling that can get in the way of your being effective. Framing the negotiation as an "ask" rather than a negotiation may work well to strengthen your resolve to engage in the first place.[2]

Another strategy for positive framing is to consider this negotiation as a win-win for both parties. This strategy fits with the collaborative orientation that reflects women's strengths. You are going into the negotiation with the frame of mind that you have prepared well and will be fully present during the process, so you can focus on ways to create a more positive experience where all parties leave having gained something.

Understanding Communication

An important element of your negotiation pre-work is to understand different aspects of communication.[3] One way to look at communication is to frame it according to three basic and underlying principles that are a core part of a practical theory called *coordinated management of meaning* (CMM).[4] The essence of the theory is that we create the social worlds that we live in through our communication. Your negotiation is part of your social world. You have the agency to create the social world in the first place and that means you have the power and agency to change it by changing how you communicate.[5]

- *Coordination:* People try to be in sync with one another and to dance to the same tune, so to speak. When we are in coordination, we "get each other" and when we are not, we feel dissonance, a feeling we do not like, so we try to fix it.

- *Coherence:* As humans, we are always trying, at a very basic level, to make sense of the world around us and to determine if it is safe. When it makes sense to us, we feel secure, and when it does not, we do not have internal coherence and we look for information that will alleviate our fears and concerns. Sometimes we grab onto the most readily available information, which may not be the most accurate.
- *Mystery:* The world is a complex place, and there is much we do not know. When we are in a situation of not knowing or understanding, we experience ambiguity, which can lead to anxiety. We need to determine how much ambiguity we can live with and remain balanced, and where the tipping point is that causes us anxiety.

These three principles interact together. Too much mystery causes dissonance, which leads to lack of coordination—we aren't sure we are in sync with our negotiating partner, for example. In preparing for a negotiation, it is good to think of these three principles as part of your preparation. You will need to be sensitive to your own feelings of angst when there is unknown information and understand that there is often much that is not known until the actual negotiation and perhaps not even then.

I have developed a communication model as an organizing framework to guide you through the different components leading to effective communication (Figure 9.1). In my experience, I have seen how communication, which can be very complex, can be misunderstood. It is a wonder that any of us can communicate effectively at any time considering all of the moving pieces that are involved. The components are foundational to understanding who you are and can be used in a variety of situations in addition to preparing for a particular negotiation.

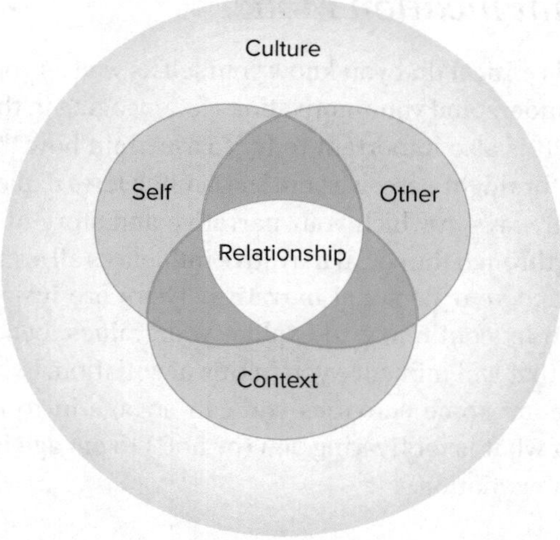

FIGURE 9.1 Communication Model

This model provides an organizing framework to use in planning for a negotiation. For each category, note information you have along with what you would like to know as you move through the negotiation. *Developed by the author in Beth Fisher-Yoshida, "Transforming Intercultural Conflict Through the Context of Relationship,"* The Sage Handbook of Conflict Communication: Integrating Theory, Research, and Practice, *2nd Edition, ed. John G. Oetzel and Stella Ting-Toomey (Thousand Oaks: Sage Publishing, 2012), p. 793; permission conveyed through Copyright Clearance Center, Inc.*

For example, self-awareness is critical to all of our interactions with others, and particularly in negotiating situations. It is lifework in that we can always improve our self-awareness because we are never in the exact same situations twice, with the same people, in the same context, negotiating the same issues. Following are ways to address each section of the model. This is one main part of the negotiation preparation checklist that has additional components listed.

Communication Model

Self: It is critical that you know yourself as well as you can to better understand your motivations for engaging in the negotiation. It is also important to try to ascertain how the other negotiator might perceive you. In Chapter 1, we explored the different ways in which your narrative and story of self are formed through the social narrative influences all around you that shape your personal narrative. There are insights you can gain by continuing to explore your values, beliefs, and morals that will influence you in this negotiation.

Here are some activities you can engage in to uncover more of what is motivating you (or not!) to engage in a particular negotiation.

Daisy Model

The Daisy Model[6] (see Figure 3.1, p. 61) is a tool from the *coordinated management of meaning* that you can use to best understand what you are bringing to the table as a negotiator. In the center of the daisy, you write in your name as the negotiator, which is the "speech act." A speech act is whatever is done or said that is the focus of examination. In this case, it is who you are as a negotiator. Then on each of the petals surrounding the center of the daisy you write one person, event, situation, value, and so on, that shapes who you are as a negotiator.

For example, maybe you had a teacher earlier in your life who helped develop who you are today, and you bring that teacher's lessons with you into your negotiation. Or maybe there was a significant event, such as moving to a new city, that exposed you to a very different environment where you had to start all over again. Perhaps you observed someone from the workplace in a negotiation, and you picked up a few tips from them. Whatever is significant for you at this moment you put on your daisy petals, knowing that your daisy petals may be subject to change.

Narrative Timeline

In Chapter 1, we discussed how your own narrative development is a combination of the social narrative around you and your personal narrative. The two have many touch points throughout your life, and it is good to know the origins and current messages about who you are as a negotiator. Looking back and mapping your timeline (Figure 9.2) allows you to see the stories you carry that will shape how you think and feel about yourself as a negotiator. Some of

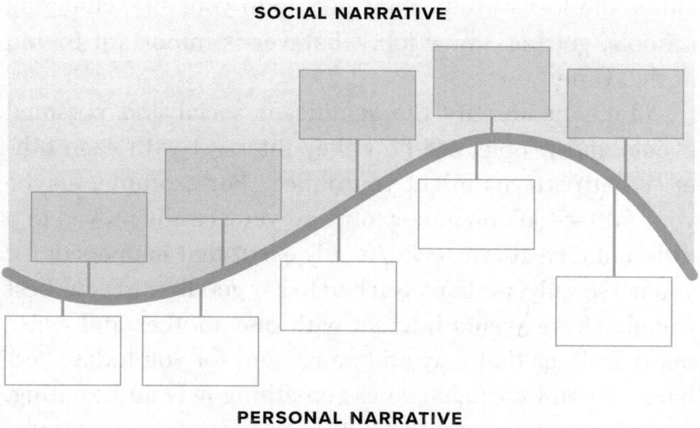

FIGURE 9.2 Narrative Timeline

We create many stories over time, and the narrative timeline, based loosely on the CMM Serpentine Model, can capture them in sequence. In this diagram, we show two sets of story flows: one for personal and the other for social narratives.
Based on the Serpentine Model used with permission by Cronen and Pearce in W. Barnett Pearce. Making Social Worlds: A Communication Perspective *(Malden: Blackwell Publishing, 2007), pp. 154–56; permission conveyed through Copyright Clearance Center, Inc.*

these stories will be helpful and give you clarity and confidence, while others will make you doubt yourself and cause you to be less likely to bring your best self forward into the negotiation.

To create your own narrative timeline, draw a line that can start at any point in time up to the present. On the top of the line, write in different dates and brief descriptions of significant events that happened around you in your social world. These can be in your family, school, community, and the larger world. You can also note people who have or had a major influence on the world around you. Under the line, write in the dates and brief descriptions of significant events that happened to you personally. These can be rites of passage, the development of meaningful friendships, the loss of important people in your life, changing schools, getting a new job, whatever is important to you at that time.

After you identify the significant social and personal events and people, see how they intersect with each other. What patterns might you notice? For example, maybe your father took on a new job, and your family moved to a different city. It is a social/family event that happened; for you personally, perhaps you had to say goodbye to your best friend. These events interact with one another and cause many feelings that may still be present for you today. Perhaps you embrace change as something new and exciting, or perhaps you dread the unknown because of its unpredictability. Perhaps it is a combination.

Now that you see the events and people, how they interact, and perhaps patterns, ask yourself the following questions:

- Which of these stories helps me be who I want to be?
- Which of these stories helps me achieve what I want to accomplish?

- Which of these stories gets in the way of my being who I want to be?
- Which of these stories gets in the way of my achieving what I want to accomplish?

The answers to these questions will help you uncover the stories you want to keep and the stories you want to change because they are stopping you from reaching your full potential.[7] They will also play in your head before, during, and after the negotiation. As part of your preparation for this negotiation and subsequent ones, it is good to strengthen the stories that work well for you and change the stories that are not serving any positive purpose.

The Other Person

As critical as it is to understand yourself, it is also just as important to understand the other person with whom you are negotiating. It is more challenging because you may or may not have known this person before. If that is the case, you will want to learn something about this person before engaging. Perhaps you know people who know her, and you can learn something about her situation and personality from them. There may also be public information that you can research to help you influence the negotiation.

You can use the same daisy model for this other person as you did for yourself. Put the person in the center of the daisy, and on the petals write in what you think is important for her personally, such as her own gains for the negotiation. On other petals, write in the other factors influencing her performance and role in the negotiation, especially where the actual decision-making lies. For example, who else is there in this other person's social world that might influence her in the negotiation? Where does she have autonomy and where is she negotiating on behalf of this other person?

I like to frame my encounters with other people in negotiations as trying to find out what I can do to help this other person be a hero. I am in it to win what I can, but at the same time, I want to support the other person as much as possible to get what he or she wants. The concept of saving face comes to mind in these situations. I want to do what I can so as not to embarrass the other person and that means avoiding causing them to lose badly. Their reputation is important to maintain, and if I have future encounters, I want to be remembered as someone who negotiated firmly and fairly. That is something that comes up when I think about my own values in negotiation and what I like to pass on to others.

Context

One of the critical factors here is that the situation you are in will influence your own mindset and behavior for the negotiation. For example, consider how you act at home as compared to how you act in the workplace. You can imagine that certain behaviors are acceptable in one place and not the other. Some behaviors are condoned, and some are condemned depending on where they take place. There are certain contextual forces at play that have been ingrained in us through our socialization process about what is right and what is wrong that lets us know these differences.[8] When we get it wrong, we know!

This will also make a difference in the strength of the relationship and whether you will interact with this other person again and, if so, how often. If it is someone at home or in your family, the potential for long-term and more emotionally involved relationships can be expected. If the workplace is the context, these may also be long-term but less involved than family and more than local vendors.

Different contexts also mean that you play different roles in each of these contexts. There are sets of rules and behaviors governing the role you play in a particular environment. You may not always be aware of these rules, but they are a deeply ingrained part of your subconscious. When you become aware of them, you may question where those ideas originated and why certain behaviors come into play.

The hierarchy model, also from the coordinated management of meaning, highlights different contexts that are in play. Each context has different moral expectations of the way we "should" be, the way we should act (Figure 9.3A). These moral forces govern and inform us when we go along with the social norms and serve to alert us if we violate them. Being more fully aware of the influences of the context provides us with more information to prepare for our negotiations.

The context can be defined as the location of the negotiations, as mentioned earlier. We might have different sets of behaviors and expectations for negotiating at home and in the workplace. We can also frame context in terms of priorities. The main priority goes at the top of the hierarchy and influences whatever is below it. These priorities can shift, causing changes in behaviors and expectations and creating the different possible scenarios that may happen during the negotiation. (Scenario planning is addressed later in this chapter.)

Figure 9.3B gives one example of how the hierarchy model might be completed when preparing for a negotiation.

Your relationship with the other person in the negotiation may become a more prominent factor that influences the negotiation. You have a role to fulfill that depends on the other person's role; the context will send messages about who holds the power. It is important to know that there are different sources of power, and positional power is one source of *power over*, meaning the person with the higher positional status will hold more power.

GROUP
What group I belong to that is most salient.
RELATIONSHIP
My relationship to the person with whom I am negotiating.
ORGANIZATION
The defining characteristics,
such as power, distribution, culture, industry.
SELF / IDENTITY
The ways in which I define myself and
aspects of my identity that are most salient.
CULTURE
The values and norms of my culture that are most salient.
SPEECH ACT
The actual communication or negotiation.

FIGURE 9.3A Hierarchy Model

This hierarchy model shows the different levels of context by category. The context at the top of the model has a stronger influence on mindset and behaviors than the levels below. The order can change over time. *Based on the Hierarchy Model used with permission by Cronen and Pearce in W. Barnett Pearce,* Making Social Worlds: A Communication Perspective *(Malden: Blackwell Publishing, 2007), pp. 189–91; permission conveyed through Copyright Clearance Center, Inc.*

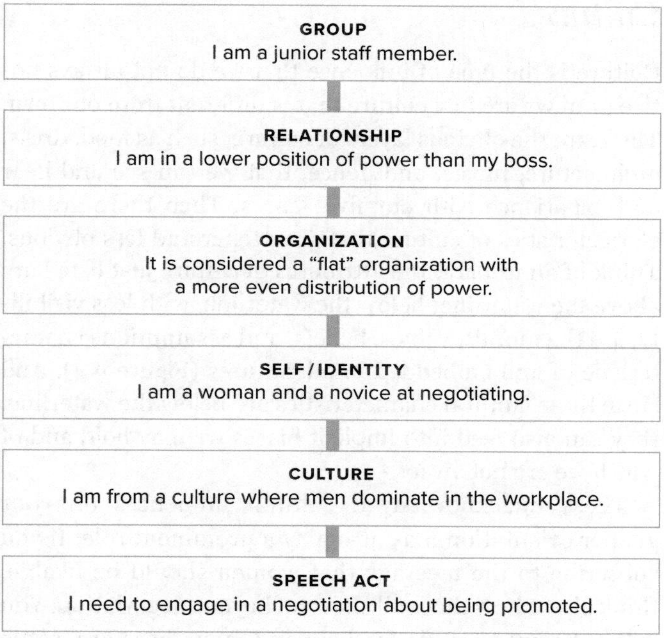
GROUP
I am a junior staff member.
RELATIONSHIP
I am in a lower position of power than my boss.
ORGANIZATION
It is considered a "flat" organization with a more even distribution of power.
SELF / IDENTITY
I am a woman and a novice at negotiating.
CULTURE
I am from a culture where men dominate in the workplace.
SPEECH ACT
I need to engage in a negotiation about being promoted.

FIGURE 9.3B Hierarchy Model Completed

This example of a completed hierarchy model shows possible responses for a junior level staff member who is preparing for a negotiation. *Based on the Hierarchy Model used with permission by Cronen and Pearce in W. Barnett Pearce,* Making Social Worlds: A Communication Perspective *(Malden: Blackwell Publishing, 2007), pp. 189–91; permission conveyed through Copyright Clearance Center, Inc.*

Culture

Culture is the type of influence that we do not always notice until we are in a culture that is different from our own. There are the obvious layers of culture, such as food, dress, architecture, music, and dance, that we can see and hear and experience with our five senses. Then there are the characteristics of culture that are deeper and less obvious. Think of an iceberg: the attributes of culture just listed are above the waterline; below the waterline, with less visibility, are the morals, values, beliefs, and assumptions characteristic of and embedded in all cultures (Figure 9.4). And since these cultural characteristics are below the waterline, they can also feed into implicit biases we may hold and of which we are not aware.[9]

These unacknowledged cultural influences on your gender orientation may also play a prominent role. If you subscribe to the message that women should be likable, think about how that will show up in your negotiation. You will not want to ruffle feathers and may, therefore, settle for less than what you deserve. You may also have a cultural orientation that you should respect your elders and, in these situations, you may not feel comfortable contradicting what an elder says. This attitude can also adversely affect how you perform in your negotiation. You may feel uncomfortable during the negotiation if you challenge him or her, or feel badly afterward that you didn't advocate for yourself as much as you needed to do.

Part of figuring out what you need to know about your negotiating partners is identifying as much as possible the cultural influences that shape them, what they will think of you, and how they will engage in the negotiation. These are aspects to look for before and during the negotiation. Of course, you will need to know your own cultural influences as well, so you can compare and contrast areas of similarity

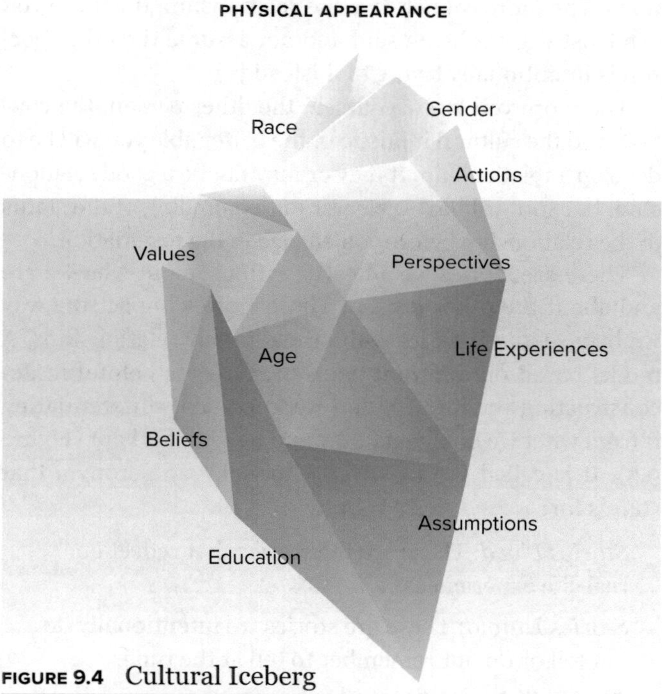

FIGURE 9.4 Cultural Iceberg

Like an iceberg, which shows only a small portion of its mass above the water line, we can see and hear what people have to say, but we don't initially know their intentions, assumptions, values or beliefs.

and difference with that of your negotiating partner.

The Role of Relationship

Negotiation is all about relationships. The quality of your relationship will affect your communication and levels of trust in the negotiation. The more familiar you are with the other party, the more likely you are to accurately interpret their behavior and comments and understand their motivations. The more cooperative the relationship, the more you can trust what is being said and not assume the other person is intentionally trying to mislead you.

The more you know yourself, the other person, the context, and the cultural influences, the better able you will be to develop a relationship. It may or may not be a good relationship, but you will have a clearer understanding of the status of the relationship before you engage in the negotiation.

There are stories we all carry with us about who we are and about the other person. These stories impact the way we behave and interact with others in our relationships. A model based on different types of stories is helpful in deconstructing the information we know and differentiating it from what we don't yet know and need to find out (Figure 9.5). It is called the LUUUUTT model,[10] an acronym that stands for:

Stories Lived: These are the stories that reflect our real-life experiences.

Stories Untold: These are stories we intentionally do not tell or do not remember to tell at the time.

Stories Unheard: These are the stories that contain messages we want others to hear; if we feel they are unacknowledged, we continue to try to communicate them.

Stories Unknown: These stories contain missing information that we do not know and need to find out.

Stories Untellable: These are the taboo stories. We do not go there. They make us very uncomfortable and telling them may have dire consequences.

Stories Told: These are the stories we tell about our lives.

Storytelling: The medium of communicating the stories, as in telephone calls, text messages, an argument, the media, and so on.

Stories Told
Women can assert.
Women are poor negotiators.
Stories Untold
Women are confused.
Women are negotiating role models.
Stories Unknown
Prevalence of successful women negotiators.
Presence of backlash.
Storytelling
At home
In the workplace
In the media
Stories Unheard
Women are negotiating successfully.
Women are not viewed well when they are bold.
Stories Lived
Women feel bold.
Women feel timid.
Stories Untellable
Women are criticized behind closed doors.
Women are not given a fair chance.

FIGURE 9.5 LUUUUTT Model

This model shows the contradictory social and organizational stories women carry about how they are expected to act in the workplace. *Adapted from the LUUUUTT Model used with permission by Cronen and Pearce in W. Barnett Pearce,* Making Social Worlds: A Communication Perspective, *212-213. (Malden: Blackwell Publishing, 2007), pp. 212–13; permission conveyed through Copyright Clearance Center, Inc.*

Look for gaps in Stories Lived and Stories Told to find out about the discrepancies causing you or another person to tell a story that is different from lived reality. If there is confusion about whether a story is untold or unknown, it is not as critical to know which category it is in as to identify that additional information gathering needs to take place.

Here is an example of using the LUUUUTT Model as part of framing a negotiation:

> *Stories Lived*: I get anxious before a negotiation. I need to spend more time preparing. I freeze if things do not go my way and try to shut down the negotiation quickly; I give up more than I should.

Stories Untold: I am not sure of what I really want from my negotiations. I rely on others when I negotiate on a team.

Stories Unheard: I really need encouragement from others. I would like to practice more role-playing before a negotiation.

Stories Unknown: I am not sure what the other party really wants from this negotiation. I am not sure how prepared the other side really is or if they are bluffing.

Stories Untellable: I failed terribly at some of my previous negotiations. I am intimidated when negotiators are very forceful and do not let me express myself.

Stories Told: I am prepared. I can establish an anchor, and I feel confident we can get what we need.

Storytelling: I tell my story in our weekly meetings and in email exchanges.

Reflecting on previous chapters, we know from Chapter 1 that we live in stories, and our narratives guide us in how we live our lives. From Chapter 2, we know that these stories are embedded in our brain pathways and that the stories we tell leave imprints in our brains that continue to influence our behavior. As we explored in Chapter 3, we know that some of these stories are deeply connected to our identity and core sense of self. Some of these stories will be easier than others to uncover, and that is important information too.

Presenting Issues

The presenting issues are what bring you to the negotiation in the first place. It does not mean these are the actual issues that will be negotiated or that are in conflict. You will try to anticipate the driving forces behind the presenting issues. We can frame the initial point of negotiation or conflict as *positions*. These are the positional stances you and the other negotiator come to the negotiation to resolve.

However, underlying these positions are the *needs* you both want to satisfy (Figure 9.6). There are many taxonomies of needs, both tangible and intangible. These are what drive us to take the positions we do because we want to satisfy our unmet needs. In the workplace, unmet needs include recognition and belonging. Some people feel they are not appreciated or acknowledged for the work they do, so their need for recognition is unmet. If you have ever had the experience of not being included in group emails or assigned to a high visibility project, you may feel left out, and your need for belonging may be unsatisfied.

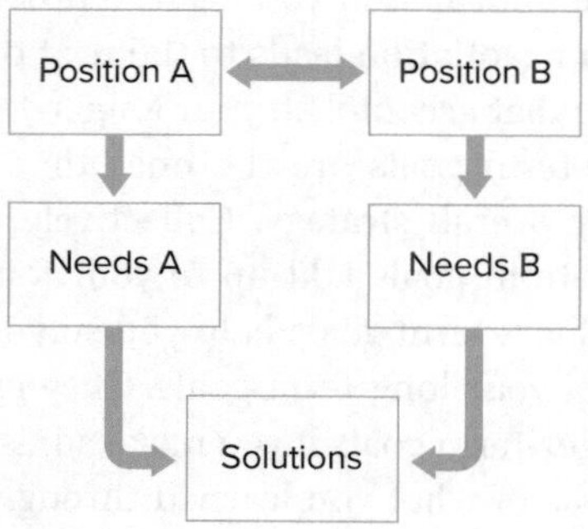

FIGURE 9.6 Positions and Needs

Our demands or initial requests are framed as positions. It is difficult to stay here and have win-win outcomes, so we need to dig down to uncover the underlying needs for more cooperative and mutually beneficial outcomes. *Based loosely on William Ury and Roger Fisher,* Getting to Yes: Negotiating Agreement Without Giving In *(New York: Penguin Books, 1981).*

At home and in your personal and romantic relationships, these same needs may go unmet. They can be caused by different behaviors and will be satisfied by different actions. It is important to know what is causing you to take the positions you take. One way of doing that is by identifying the unmet needs fueling these positions that can lead to conflict if unresolved.

Short- and Long-Term Goals

It is important to differentiate between short-term and long-term goals. Short-term goals can focus on what you want to achieve in this particular negotiation. You may or may not achieve all the outcomes you seek in this first-round negotiation. Instead, you may be laying the groundwork for subsequent negotiations. If building a relationship or collecting information was your short-term goal for this first negotiation, then you are ahead if you establish rapport and gather the information you need to proceed. This implies that each negotiation leads to the next one in a series of negotiations that accomplish your longer-term goals.

The longer-term goals are the ones that more directly link to your overall strategy. Collectively, the series of smaller, short-term goals add up to your long-term goals (Figure 9.7). Short-term goals help you stay the course toward achieving your long-term goals. They can also influence your longer-term goals if you make adjustments along the way because of what you learned through the smaller, short-term negotiations.

One way of thinking about short- and long-term goals, and how short-term goals feed into long-term goals, is to think about the level of engagement of your negotiating partner. If you are challenged in bringing your negotiating partner to the table before you can even make your ask, then as a short-term goal, just beginning the conversation

SHORT-TERM GOALS	LONG-TERM GOALS
1. Get an appointment to speak with your manager or other influencer.	Get a promotion to a management-level position.
2. Research the job requirements for such a position.	
3. Share some of your accomplishments with your manager and ask for more responsibility.	
4. Ask for the promotion.	

FIGURE 9.7 Short- and Long-Term Goals

Negotiations may be one-off events or they may be a series of events leading to fulfilling long-term goals. Framing each negotiation to achieve a short-term goal allows you to continue to build a relationship, while amassing these short-term goals to satisfying a long-term goal.

can be a win. You are building rapport and developing the relationship so that the long-term goal is more within reach than when you started. Being able to frame these short-term gains as wins provides motivation to continue on the longer journey of achieving long-term goals.

Best Alternative to a Negotiated Agreement (BATNA)

You need to know how important this particular negotiation is to you, and one way of assessing its level of importance to your overall strategy is knowing your BATNA[11]—the Best Alternative to a Negotiated Agreement. In other words, if you have viable alternatives, this particular negotiation is less important, and you can take bigger risks. If it does not work out, you still have other options.

For example, say that you are seeking employment, and you receive several job offers. If the job offers have similar value to you, you can negotiate for more benefits, such as a higher salary, a more senior title, or more vacation days. You feel you can do this because if it doesn't work out, you have other viable job offers.

However, if you do not have any other good alternatives, then this negotiation carries more weight, putting more pressure on you to do well. You will need to manage your emotions and take fewer risks because you want to succeed in this negotiation. That means you will be more willing to accept the salary, title, and vacation days that are offered to you. You do not want to allow your negotiating partner to see how important the job is to you. You are also trying to determine the other person's BATNA, both beforehand and during the negotiation. You might look for cues, such as how long the position has been open, or when the position starts, to let you know how easy or difficult it has been to fill the position and how eager the hiring manager is to have it filled. This can inform you that they are in a weaker negotiating position because their BATNA is weak, especially if they do not have other viable candidates.

In identifying reasonable options to this negotiation to have a more fully informed sense of your BATNA, you will probably want to be as expansive and creative in your thinking as possible. Go back to your unmet needs and not just to your positions to think innovatively about how to satisfy those needs. Your positions are one way but not the *only* way to meet your unmet needs. Determining other options gives you a wider playing field in which to negotiate. Identify what happens if the negotiation does not happen or does not turn out well. What might happen instead? What other options do I have to meet my unmet needs?

Zone of Proximal Agreement (ZOPA)

Just as it is important to know your BATNA in a negotiation context, it is also important to know your ZOPA—your Zone of Proximal Agreement.[12] This is the bargaining range of your negotiation. Both parties must have an initial offer that fits within the bargaining range, or there is no negotiation. Your low or least amount and highest upper limits determine your bargaining range, and this range needs to overlap with the other person's bargaining range. The area that overlaps is known as the ZOPA (Figure 9.8). If there is no overlap in your bargaining range, there is no negotiation.

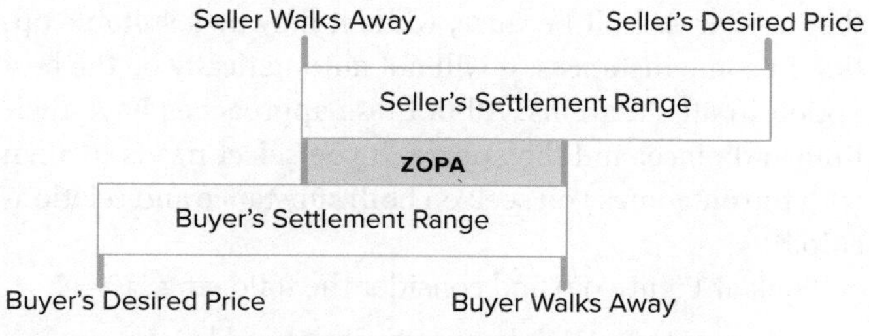

FIGURE 9.8 Zone of Possible Agreement (ZOPA)

This zone, or bargaining range, will let you know as a negotiator whether you are close enough in asking and selling prices, for example, for there to even be a negotiation. If your initial offers are way outside of this range, then there may be too big a gap for a negotiation. *Katie Shonk. "How to Find the ZOPA in Business Negotiations." Blog entry.*

Your Approach to a Negotiation

There are different ways to approach your negotiation. Once you make the decision about your approach—and it should be intentional and not your default mode—all other aspects need to align. These include how much information you share, your tone, your willingness to compromise, and so on.

One way of framing the different approaches you might take in your negotiation is to think of two axes that represent the level of assertiveness, or how much you push your own agenda, and the level of cooperation, or how much you care for and satisfy the other person's agenda. Together, these axes and five approaches to negotiation are known as the Dual Concern Model (Figure 9.9).[13] Each approach is good in some situations and not in others.

Since every approach has consequences, you will want to align your choice of approach with the consequences you are willing to accept and then take responsibility for them. It is less effective to operate on autopilot and use the approach that is your default because, while it may be a suitable option in some instances, it will not automatically be the best option in all situations. All of these approaches have their time and place, and the approach you select needs to align with the outcomes you seek on both substance and relationship.[14]

Look at Figure 9.9 and consider the following:

- *Competing*: High in assertiveness and low in cooperation (towards the left on the X-axis and at the top of the Y-axis) indicates that in competing, it is all about you and not the other person. You push your agenda, and this includes not sharing information or intentionally misleading with the information you share. Keep in mind that competition has a win-lose

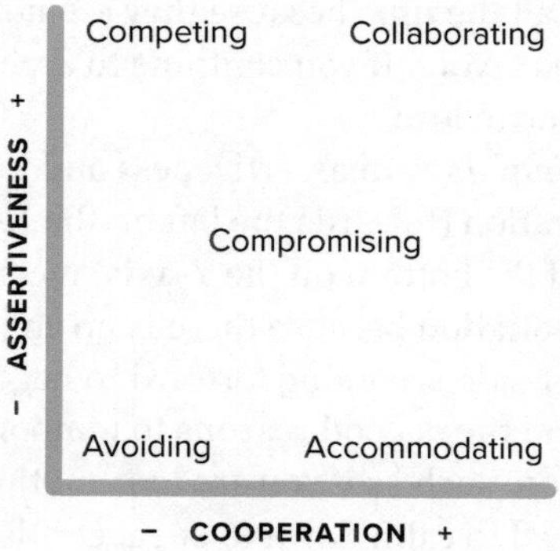

FIGURE 9.9 Dual-Concern Model

There are several approaches to take when engaging in negotiation, and each has its own strategies, tactics, and consequences. It is important to explore the different approaches and select the one to use rather than using the same approach by default. *Based on the work of Dean Pruitt, 1983.*

dynamic, and the person who loses will not be happy. If you continue to use competition as your default approach, there may be backlash. This approach does not have a relationship orientation.

- *Accommodating*: Low in assertiveness and high in cooperation (towards the right on the X-axis and at the bottom on the Y-axis) is the opposite of competitive in that you are more concerned about how the other party does in the negotiation than with how you fare. It could be that the issues are not that important to you or that you are trying to do a favor for the other party, and expecting favors in return. Remember that unless you state your intentions for accommodating openly, the other person may think this is your normal behavior and will expect these favors all the time because they are not thinking of them as favors. If you continue to accommodate, you continue to lose.

- *Avoiding*: Low in assertiveness and low in cooperation (towards the left on the X-axis and toward the bottom on the Y-axis) means there is no negotiation because there is no engagement. Neither side is coming forward to negotiate. There are sometimes good reasons to temporarily avoid the situation, such as if you are too emotionally heated and need to calm down to engage satisfactorily, or you are missing information that is necessary for you to negotiate. However, avoidance means that the issues that need to be negotiated are not getting resolved, and eventually you will need to engage in a negotiation to address them. You may also want to consider a neutral third party, such as a mediator, to intervene in a facilitated negotiation.
- *Compromising*: In the middle both, in assertiveness and in cooperation, may be the best you can do in some cases. Compromises are partial wins because both parties win some of what they want and lose other demands. While it is satisfactory in some situations and may be a good first step toward eventual collaboration, it is not useful to continue to think of this as the ultimate outcome.
- *Collaborating*: High in assertiveness and high in cooperation would be the ideal standard if we could all have our ways. Both sides win, you build good relationships, and everyone walks away satisfied. The downside to collaboration is that it requires trust that may not be there, it takes a lot of time and effort, and you may not have those resources. It involves openly sharing information, and not everything needs to be shared even in collaborative negotiations.

Scenario Planning

When you do scenario planning, you are trying to anticipate the possible ways the negotiation will play out. You want to plan for as many possibilities as you can envision based on what you know about all of the other aspects of the negotiation listed above. In one scenario, you can map out like so: if I say "A" and he says "B," then I will respond with "C." Or if I say "A" and he says "D," I will respond with "E," or something along those lines (Figure 9.10).

You will probably not be able to figure out every possible scenario because there is always the chance that some new and unexpected piece of information or development will enter into the negotiation. In this situation, you will want to buy yourself time to compose yourself and quickly decide the direction you should take.

To buy yourself more time to think and compose yourself, it is always good to have stock phrases and questions at the ready so that you do not freeze. Some examples could be: "Oh, that is interesting. Can you tell me more about it?"

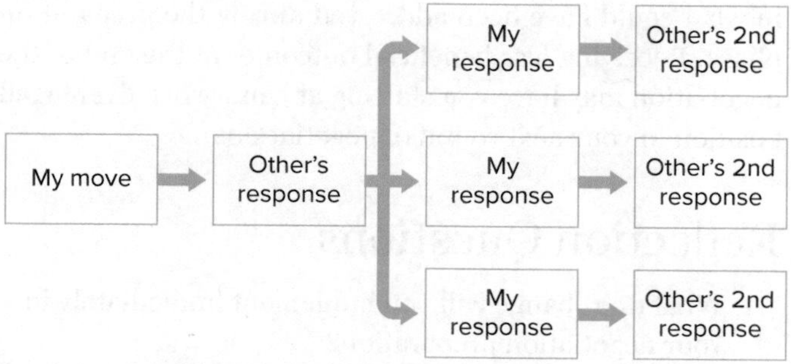

FIGURE 9.10 Scenario Planning

Preparing for a negotiation is critical, as is identifying possible directions the negotiation can take. This is framed as scenario planning. For example, if the other party says "A," you will be agile enough to know how to counter.

or “I was not expecting that request. Can you tell me more about what is prompting it?” While the other person is responding, you are gaining both new information and precious time to regain your control over yourself and your role in the negotiation. You are asserting your agency and taking back control of your negotiation flow in response to what may have been meant to throw you off track.

You do not need to go it alone during the preparation phase. It is good practice to engage others who are either also learning along with you or have the skills you want to master. In addition, there are several materials to review, such as books, TED Talks, videos, research papers, and more.

Preparation is key to a successful negotiation. At times, you may feel you do not have the time to invest in a thorough preparation. If that happens, ask yourself to reflect on what happens if the negotiation does not go well because you weren’t ready. You may have lacked emotional control at some point, there may have been moments of being stuck because the negotiation took an unexpected turn, or the outcomes were much less than desirable. This means you will need to invest more in picking up the pieces afterwards in what could have been addressed during the preparation phase. Receiving less beneficial outcomes at the end of the negotiation may have you starting at a more disadvantaged position in your next round of negotiations.

Reflection Questions

1. What one change will you implement immediately in your negotiation preparation?
2. In what areas do you need to strengthen your negotiation preparation?
3. How will you go about strengthening your negotiation preparation?

10

Lessons to Take with You: The Negotiation Process

You have done all of the pre-work necessary to engage in this negotiation and to have the confidence that you can manage well whatever comes your way. The script that you prepared is the one that should be playing in your head!

The Negotiation Process

A negotiation has many components, and one important part of the information-gathering you will do is to determine the accuracy of your preparation. You want to confirm what you anticipated and determine what information needs to be modified. It could be that some of the information is incorrect, but chances are that you correctly identified some aspects that will support you through this process.

Communication

All negotiations require communication. The more collaborative your negotiation, the more openly you will share information. This requires a combination of good listening and good questioning skills. Listening well helps you hear both what is being said and what is not being said—the messages being communicated from facial expressions and gestures.

You will listen to all that is being said to distill the information you need to move the negotiation along. Try also to listen at the feeling level, which includes what is explicitly or implicitly communicated. You want to know how the words being spoken affect the person speaking them from the feeling level. You want to be attuned to your own reaction to the information at the cognitive and feeling levels. Listening at the feeling level also provides an opportunity for you to show empathy, which can be done verbally or nonverbally.

If someone is quick to respond that what you are asking for cannot be given, and their tone is abrupt, they cross their arms across their chest, and they look stern, chances are that you hit a nerve with your request. Your negotiating partner is not actually voicing an emotion, but everything from their tone of voice to their body language is screaming emotions. If you encounter such a reaction, you have the opportunity to show empathy and proceed slowly, paying attention to shifts in their demeanor. Asking questions can assist you in this.

Asking questions serves several purposes. One is to get the other party talking and sharing information. In negotiation, information is power. Asking questions also helps you decide whether the assumptions you made going into the negotiation were accurate (or not). Asking questions is also good because doing so buys you time, especially if you become unnerved and need to compose yourself.[1]

If your negotiating partner is not forthcoming with information, it is a good strategy to begin with closed questions that require short, usually factual, responses. Once your negotiating partner is talking and seemingly more relaxed and trusting, it will be easier to transition into open questions. Both types of questions will glean useful information. It is up to you to be strategic in how you ask the questions to keep the conversation going, as you continue to build rapport and trust.

Figure 10.1 is a typology of questions you may use. Feel free to create your own that you feel comfortable using for each of the categories.

CATEGORIES	QUESTIONS / STATEMENTS
Clarification	I am curious why you say that. Can you help me understand? How do you see this relating to our discussion?
Probe Assumptions	What could we assume instead? How can you verify or disprove that assumption?
Probe Reasons and Evidence	What would be an example? What do you think causes this to happen?
Viewpoints and Perspectives	What would be an alternative? Would you explain why it is beneficial and who benefits?
Probe Implications and Consequences	What generalizations can you make? What are the consequences of that assumption?
About the Question	What was the point of this question? (I am not sure I understand the point of this question.) Why do you think I asked that question?

FIGURE 10.1 Question Typology

There are many direct and indirect benefits to asking good questions. It can buy you time, provide valuable information, and keep the negotiations flowing, so have one or two questions ready to use at any moment. *Created by the author.*

Managing Emotions

Much has been written about emotional intelligence, which is a combination of you managing your own emotions, including your reactions to the other party, and managing the relational dynamics. Managing your emotions can be difficult when you are in the middle of a negotiation, especially if it becomes heated or you are talking about sensitive issues that are meaningful to both parties. Neuroscience research shows that when we are able to maintain a calm state, we listen more attentively because our calmness releases positive hormones called *neurotransmitters*.[2]

It is important, therefore, to have a regular practice of techniques to calm your nerves and regain composure. It is not a good idea to start a meditation routine in the middle of a difficult negotiation! Some people do exercise to release tension, others meditate, some listen to soothing music, some relax with friends, or others do deep breathing. Then, when in these challenging situations, think of a trigger, such as a sound or a color, that will bring you back to that peaceful state you achieve when doing these calming activities.

An interesting way to frame this practice is *going to the balcony*.[3] Since you may not be able to physically leave the room, you can emotionally detach by leaving that environment and taking a meta-perspective. It is a way to emotionally disengage, re-center, and then re-engage. Do not stay on the balcony because then even though it may feel good, you will not be engaged in the negotiation. Come back to the negotiation with a new sense of calm, focus, and energy.

It is difficult to manage emotions when you slip back into *unwanted repetitive patterns* (URPs) that are characteristic of destructive dynamics.[4] Recognizing patterns in your behavior is important because it provides information for you about what your typical actions and responses are and whether they bring satisfactory or unsatisfactory results. If you know in advance that the other person might do something to trigger a URP, you can think about ways to calm your nerves and re-center so you do not get triggered.[5]

One more point to consider is the role of your brain during this time. In Chapter 2, we explored how your brains budget the amount of energy you will need in your daily life, but negotiations may call for additional resources, causing extra strain and stress on your system. To avoid the added stress, be sure to build in rejuvenating breaks so you do not wear yourself down. In addition, because you are a social being, your brain and the brain of your negotiating partner will also be busy communicating with one another during the negotiation. Anticipate some of the effects this activity will have on you, especially emotionally and in terms of spending energy, and plan accordingly.

You can find more in-depth information about emotions in Chapter 5. In that chapter, we looked at emotions from the context of what happens within a family. The lessons and information there can be applied more broadly as well.

Placing an Anchor

Just as a ship uses an anchor to stay in place, the person who initiates a negotiation places their own anchor. There are different opinions as to whether it is better to place the anchor or be the first to respond to the anchor. Those in favor of placing the anchor believe that it sets the stage for the negotiation, and everything that follows is in reaction to the anchor. You are then setting the initial offer or claim.[6]

Those in favor of not placing the anchor, but going second, so to speak, believe that whoever sets the anchor reveals information that will be helpful. You always have the choice as to whether to respond directly to the given anchor or to change the conversation and place a new anchor. This can be done tactfully by stating something such as, "Before we get to that, I would like to first establish . . ." You are not disagreeing that what was already stated will be addressed, you are just delaying *when* it gets addressed.

Staying on Track, Maintaining Control, and Buying Time

It is important that you stay in control of your own performance during the negotiation. The other party may be supporting you, as in a collaborative negotiation, or trying to unnerve you, as in a more competitive negotiation. Your self-talk in these moments makes all the difference as to your mindset and what you believe you will be able to achieve.

There may also be power dynamics in play if the other person is trying to exert power over you. If you feel sensations of being manipulated, the other person could be using power dynamics. Notice these moves and have counter moves so that you do not succumb to these tactics. It is good to know various tactics that are used in negotiations so that you can recognize them and have a counter. You may also use some of these tactics yourself.

A tactic used to establish or maintain control is rushing the negotiation—negotiating at a pace that is not comfortable for the other party. This tactic may cause you to feel you are losing control. You will want to set and maintain a pace that is good for you. Another power tactic may be to dismiss something as having no value, when in actuality it may be very valuable, but that level of importance is something not to be revealed to the other party.

Before beginning a negotiation, you will need to have something ready to use that will buy you time and give you a chance to compose yourself if you feel you are losing control. It could be something you say to yourself, an image, or maybe even asking an open question to seek more information. Of course, you always have the option of calling for a break to physically remove yourself from that space for a few minutes to regain your composure or to rejuvenate. Be sure to agree, up front, that periodic breaks will be taken throughout the negotiation and can be set in advance or called for when either party requests one.

Acting Out the Scenarios

During your preparation, you outlined several scenarios that might happen. Listen for the clues as to which direction the other party is taking. It may or may not be exactly as you envisioned, but it may be close enough that you can continue on your path. Also, pay attention to any directions the conversation is taking that you did not anticipate. Enter into this part of the negotiation with curiosity and be prepared to ask a clarifying question to get more information and time for you to figure out a response that will keep you working on your path toward your desired outcomes.

All of the work you did during the negotiation preparation can be more effective if you also manage the negotiation process well. One of the most critical parts is managing yourself during the negotiation. This means you are listening well for what *is* being said and what *is not* being said, at both the content and feeling levels. It means you are managing your emotions and using triggers that take you to a relaxed mental and physical state. It also means you can be agile in the moment and pivot regardless of whatever comes your way, including buying time to regain your composure.

Reflection Questions

1. What tactic(s) will you use to regain emotional composure during a negotiation?
2. Which communication technique do you want to integrate into your negotiation practice?
3. How will you identify the needs of your negotiating partner?

11

Lessons to Take with You: Post Negotiation

You've completed the first two phases of the negotiation—preparation and process. What happens after the negotiation is equally important. Here is where the implementation must be done, and it is critical that all are on the same page at the end. In addition, it is critical to continue developing the relationship to ensure that all are committed and reliable. Therefore, it is important to develop and carry out an implementation plan for what was agreed to during the negotiation.

Post-Negotiation Implementation

Every negotiation takes twists and turns, and it is difficult to keep track of every piece of information shared. It is important, therefore, to keep a summary of mini-agreements made along the way and areas of follow-up that were identified. This is something that can be done immediately following the negotiation so that all parties leave with a shared understanding of agreements and next steps. It is also important to follow up shortly after the conclusion of the negotiation to make sure that, after a short time away, everyone is still on the same page.

Follow-Up Summary

If you fail to do the follow-up summary, it is possible that not everyone left the table with the same understanding. Information has a way of being received and interpreted differently by different people, and it is to your advantage to clarify to avoid any differences in understanding. This step is critical in ensuring successful implementation following the negotiation. It is also useful because when negotiators leave the table and share the results with others, they may face a whole host of reactions that cause them to waiver on some agreements. They may look for wiggle room on the interpretation. That is why you want to lock in what was agreed to by all directly involved parties.

If it turns out that a new consideration surfaces, it will need to be presented to the other party. If both parties agree to this new consideration, fine. If not, it is important to honor the initial agreement or your word and reputation will suffer, and that will make it more difficult the next time around. If the agreement is not secure, there will be a misunderstanding the next time around.

Developing an Action Plan

The action plan may come directly at the end of the negotiation or, if both parties agree, shortly thereafter. It is important to include a description of the action steps, the responsible parties, the outcomes desired, the time frame of when it will be accomplished, and the resources needed (Figure 11.1). It is also important to include a plan for how the information will continue to be shared and how communication will continue during the implementation phases.

It is important to determine in advance how disagreements will be managed. Since there is a good chance that not everything will go according to plan, you will need to have clearly defined actions for how to handle disputes.[1] If you know in advance how you plan to address conflicts, disagreements will more likely be managed well and not escalated. You want to address small problems before they grow bigger and threaten to overturn all of the good work

ACTION STEPS	TIME FRAME	LEAD PERSON	RESOURCES	NEXT STEPS
1.				
2.				
3.				

FIGURE 11.1 Action Planning

In order to internalize a new learning, it is important to set up an action plan so that you hold yourself accountable to how and when you will implement this new learning. An action plan will increase your chances of mastering this new concept or skill.

accomplished thus far. In some cases, third parties will be called in to mediate or arbitrate, and that is good to know in advance.

Building a Relationship

Before and during the negotiation, you have chances to build a relationship with the person with whom you are negotiating. Implementation of the agreements is another point at which it is important to consider the nature of your relationship. For these actions to be taken the way they were planned, it is important to trust that all involved parties have the best intentions and will carry out what they committed to do. Identify in advance how you will keep up the flow of communication and determine what else can be value-added so that you continue down a constructive and collaborative path.

Locating and Supplying Resources

When you are planning the action steps, it is important to identify the resources you will need. It is also good to come to some agreement on the sourcing of these resources. Either side may make suggestions that can be helpful, and third parties can be involved too. You want to make sure there are no issues about where resources originate or who is supplying them, and these things are good to clarify upfront.

Preparing for Further Negotiations

First, you will need to congratulate yourself that you have come this far! You may need to engage again to get to the next phase of this current work and have subsequent negotiations. You may enter into a totally new realm and will need to initiate and prepare for a new set of negotiations.

This is a great time to take a step back and reflect on what you have learned and accomplished thus far. These lessons learned are valuable to you for your future negotiations. The information will reinforce your positive self-story of who you are as a negotiator and give the added boost of confidence you need to keep going. It will also highlight any red flags you noticed that you want to address in advance of your next negotiation. Whatever you do, be sure to focus on your strengths and on what went well before even acknowledging that something was less than desired. It is important to continue to build on your strengths and then address and compensate for areas that require more learning and attention.

Reflection Questions

1. What is your main strategy for ensuring that there is appropriate follow-up to the negotiation?
2. What tactics will you use to stay on track?
3. Who else will you call on to support you in implementing the negotiation agreement?

12

Going Forward

We will now consider ways of putting all of this information to use in thinking through strategic approaches to moving forward in our negotiations. Chapters 9, 10, and 11 provided processes to follow in the three main stages of any negotiation. The preparation stage, covered in Chapter 9, included self-work and can be ongoing, since we can always learn more about ourselves. We will never be in the same exact situation, with the same people, negotiating the same issues twice. Certain elements may feel repetitive, but we are not the same people from one minute to the next, so how we engage with others will not be the same.

There are different ways to continue the journey of self-discovery and improvement. We have explored changing the narrative in our heads to one that is more supportive, constructive, and encouraging. We can do this work in isolation by reflecting on previous interactions, noting the successes, and things that may not have gone so well. Notice I did not use the word "failure" because from every "lesser success," there are lessons to be learned, so not all bad.[1]

We can also learn with others because we are social beings, and we learn in groups.[2] Becoming more skilled and knowledgeable about negotiation does not need to be a lonely experience. Learning with others can be fun and can actually expedite the learning process.

It is good to find role models who excel at communication and negotiation, those who walk the talk and exemplify the way we aspire to be in our own negotiations. Going through this process helps us create new tracks that will lead us closer to successful negotiations that are in alignment with how we define success. We will make new emotional predictions that will show up in new emotional states. One example of this is switching out fear of a negotiation to positive anticipation. Yes!

Setting Boundaries

It is important to set boundaries for yourself ahead of a negotiation to know where you will and will not go. Knowing these boundaries will also help you identify the times when you need to end a negotiation and walk away. This can include being in a stalemate, where you feel it is no longer worth your efforts to continue negotiating. You may feel that you have exhausted the tactics you prepared for the negotiation, and you have no alternative but to exit. You may also feel that the other party is not negotiating in good faith.

A simple, three-part rubric might help you decide when to negotiate and when to walk away. *Engage* because there are numerous and open possibilities; *walk away* when it is no longer beneficial, or there is a stalemate; *run away* when you are in compromising and dangerous circumstances. Once you decide which of the three positions you are in, there are follow-up steps to take to carry through with engaging, walking away, or running away.

If you decide to engage, you proceed with the preparation, process, and post-negotiation steps covered in Chapters 9 through 11. If you decide to walk away, it is because you identified your BATNA, which was covered in Chapter 9, and it was more beneficial for you to pursue other means that better serve your interests. If you decide to run away, you need to determine if the threat was serious enough to report to someone who has the power to do something about it.

Keep in mind that even if a negotiation ended before the issues being negotiated were resolved, it does not mean the negotiation is completely over. Maybe some time needs to pass for you and the other party to reevaluate your options, reconsider your BATNA, and then re-engage. This is a good idea to keep open as a possibility. Prior to making the commitment to even reconsider, you might also want to identify what needs to change for you to have this reconsideration. When those criteria are met, you can re-engage.

If the other party reaches out to you first, it is a good idea to question what caused them to reconsider. If the reasons given are acceptable, then get back to it. In the meantime, it is also good for you to have a reason why you have reconsidered if you are the one initiating a new negotiation. Being an agile negotiator means that you are prepared and ready to pivot. It does not mean you need to drop everything and jump if they beckon. But it does mean you need to be ready to seize the opportunity when it presents itself to you.

Motivation

Negotiations can be both tiring and emotionally draining. We need to think of ways to stay motivated because that will give us energy to continue to pursue what we need to do to be prepared and to persevere.

It is important to identify short-term gains because the immediacy of seeing progress is a motivator in itself. In the preparation phase of our negotiation process, it is important to identify small gains that eventually and cumulatively equal big, significant gains. Understanding how each component of a negotiation or each small negotiation is part of a longer-term process helps us be patient and energized. The quick rewards also help us to create new habits because we see that our efforts work, and the positive reinforcement makes us want to repeat the experience.[3] These are the internal rewards we glean for ourselves based on our hard work and performance.

There are also external motivators that fuel our energy to continue honing our skills. These can be in the form of receiving praise from others on how well we negotiated or how much we accomplished. These external motivators can also come in the way of how we compare ourselves to others. If we see someone performing well and notice there is something that we also do in our negotiations, it is confirmation that we are on the right track for improving our skills.

Because our brains record these positive experiences, we need to keep up the positive self-talk as a way of encouraging ourselves and also imprint these good skills and experiences into our brains. It will help these pathways become habits and we will be on an upward spiral of experience and improvement.

Another motivator might be to think about incentives along the way. It is useful to identify mini-rewards for mini-achievements to stay on track. For example, stating the small wins as we go along will help us make note of them and provide positive reinforcement to make the methods we used to gain these successes into new habits. It is also getting us to achieve a balance in risk and reward: try a new technique and create a reward. Changing our negotiating habits can be hard work, so rewarding ourselves for overcoming any resistance we might be putting up is a worthwhile endeavor.

Implementing Correctives Along the Way

There will be several opportunities along the way to self-correct if the negotiations are not going exactly as you want. Kennedy and Kray[4] identify several categories in which you can consider how to make these corrections: cognitive, motivational, and paradigmatic.

Cognitive

- *Adopt a growth mindset.* Carol Dweck[5] notes that a growth mindset and a fixed mindset are different. In a fixed mindset, we try to prove our ability. Whereas in a growth mindset, we change our ability through learning.[6] It is being open to learning and changing that is key. If there is something that is not working well for us, we need to see why and learn new skills and approaches. Every negotiation is an opportunity for learning and improvement and accepting that the skills we learn are malleable, and our brains are able to be shaped to learn new skills because of neuroplasticity.[7]
- *Express implicit biases.* We all have implicit biases that are usually hidden from us until we are in situations that cause us to become aware of them because they get in the way or are exposed.[8] This can be especially true if we make judgments about someone based on gender, race, age or other demographic criteria, or judgments are made about us for the same reasons. It is a good time to check our assumptions and self-correct to move us forward in a fair and positive way.
- *Focus on shared identities.* We all have our own sense of identity, and we all have multiple groups to which we belong. If we continue framing negotiation as a relational activity, we can find an identity group that we have in common with our negotiating partner. It is important to connect on a human level and finding common ground.

Motivational

- *Install norms to minimize identity threat.* Competent women can be a threat for some, especially if they lean toward being more assertive than not. This can also be the case if women have higher positional power. Establishing norms that all can feel comfortable with and protected by will keep people engaged in the negotiation while reducing any potential threat they may feel.
- *Advocate for other women.* Having the mindset that there is enough for everyone makes it easier to advocate for others. We do not need to think that there is room for only one woman, and I am out if I support the other woman. Instead, we can think of ample space and roles for all and be a good advocate for other women, to give voice to those whose voices are quiet or have been silenced.
- *Display non-threatening interpersonal styles.* Connecting with others on the human level and exhibiting empathy and warmth are means of engaging. We create an atmosphere where others can also feel comfortable. It is not a sign of weakness and if it is read that way, the preparation and how we handle ourselves during the negotiating process will correct that interpretation.

Paradigmatic

- *Gender paradigms.* As we have discussed earlier, traditional ways of negotiating have been set up to favor culturally condoned male styles of interaction. Women have strengths in building longer-term relationships, so if we frame negotiation from that paradigm, we can shift the focus from being only this negotiation to being this negotiation in the context of a longer relationship.

- *Building capital.* Too often, negotiation outcomes are based on economic gains, and there is so much more involved in successful negotiations. Building relational and social capital is also important. If we reflect on our relationships that have continued to grow over the years and that have reciprocity embedded within them, we can see that this happened with a long-term focus and not one-off encounters.
- *Broaden the definition of negotiation.* If we think of negotiating as a form of relational communicating, the definition broadens. Here is where we can differentiate "small n" negotiations from "big N" negotiations. "Small n" negotiations are the everyday, less consequential negotiations we have on an ongoing basis. The "big N" negotiations are about more serious negotiations with bigger effects and consequences.

Have Fun

I cannot say that this is a requirement, but it should be. If we think of negotiating as building relationships with others, it makes sense that we can have fun in the process of learning, growing together socially, and getting what we need through negotiating. Please be fair to yourselves and reward yourself constantly for all of the effort you will put into honing your negotiation skills. Keep moving forward, and enjoy your negotiations.

Reflection Questions

1. How will you know whether it is worth your while to engage in a negotiation?
2. How will you keep yourself motivated to endure?
3. In what ways will you make your negotiations fun?

PART 4

CASE STUDIES

In this section, we will explore three case studies and set the context, describe the characters involved, and take you through the three phases of preparing for the negotiation, the negotiation process, and post negotiation. Each case study utilizes some of the tools presented in Chapters 9, 10, and 11. As presented here, the case studies show one way the negotiation could develop. There are several ways negotiations can occur in real life.

13

Case Study 1: Internal or External Hire?

Everyone who works outside the home has discovered that negotiating is almost a daily reality. Sometimes the issues are small and the stakes are low. At other times, as in the situation described here, the issues are critically important to both parties.

Shared Information

Min has worked in a consumer goods company for a little more than four years. She is on a team in the tech division supporting one of the brands, and she has received good performance reviews. A managerial position opened up in her division, and while Min did not have any managerial experience, she felt confident that her technical skills would strengthen her application. After 12 years working in the tech world as an individual contributor, Min was ready for this next phase of her career.

Imani was an external applicant from the information security division of a logistics company. Imani has almost 18 years of tech and information technology experience as an individual contributor and a few years' experience supervising others. Imani was ready to take on more managerial responsibilities and strategically use this position as a stepping stone to a more senior position at headquarters.

The director of the technology and information security division offered the manager position to Imani. Min was a member of one of several teams that would now report to Imani. Min was hurt by not receiving the promotion, and she couldn't understand why Imani's qualifications were stronger than hers. She acknowledged that she did not have supervisory experience, but she applied for the position to develop those skills as the next step in her career advancement. She was familiar with the company, was a diligent worker, and stayed long hours, even working on weekends during crunch time with no complaints.

Imani did not initially know that a member of one of her teams, Min, had also applied for the position. However, there was a chill in the air between her and Min that she didn't understand. Min followed all directions given to her and was an independent worker, but if Imani had to describe it, she would call Min's behavior passive aggressive. Imani did not feel comfortable talking to anyone about this because she wasn't sure about the alliances in the division, and she didn't want to make matters worse. However, something needed to be done if she was going to be a successful manager and develop cohesion among the teams.

Min realizes that while she is disappointed about not receiving the promotion, she needs to know why so she can continue to develop and work on the skills she lacks. She doesn't feel comfortable sharing this with Imani because she is not sure whether Imani will support her or feel threatened by her since Min has been with the company for a longer time.

Imani and Min are at a bit of an impasse, and the air is tense. Others in the division notice this chill between them, and some are aware that Min also applied for the same position. They do not want to interfere, but they really wish Imani and Min would find a way to work it out because it is affecting all of them.

Min's Private Information

Min is a conscientious person and takes great pride in being thorough in her work. When she is asked for her recommendation on a new technology, system upgrade, or vendor to work with, Min spends extra time researching and putting all of the details into her reports. She feels that this is what a responsible contributor does and that others appreciate and trust her work because of it. Anything less would be unacceptable.

Min has difficulty speaking up in team meetings, especially when there are multiple teams at the division level or when the team is presenting to a business unit. She prefers to compile her research report and let the evidence speak for itself. However, she knows that a presentation with her recommendations is a necessary part of the process and something she needs to master before being able to grow in her career.

She has received feedback that her presentations are overly detailed, and she notices that those in senior positions become impatient. Min can be on the fifth slide of a deck of 30, and senior management rushes her along asking for the conclusion before Min can successfully build a case. She assumes everyone wants to know all of the details leading up to her recommendation. When managers become impatient, Min becomes flustered, and her reaction is to dive even more deeply into the details of every slide.

Currently, she feels slighted that the managerial position was given to Imani, an external candidate. Min heard rumors that Imani knows someone at the top and that was why she was given the position. Min believes her thoroughness and great attention to detail should have strengthened her candidacy. Maybe it did, but not enough to get this promotion. She likes working in this organization and feels comfortable and committed to staying. Min knows that there are areas she needs to improve—like communication and influencing others—based on some of the feedback she received from past performance reviews.

Min is well-liked but is sometimes described as mousy and technical. She's not sure what that means exactly, but she knows she needs to speak up more and let her opinions be known. Min thinks it irresponsible to speak up without evidence to support her claims. Yet it seems she is expected to be more concise when she communicates. This is uncomfortable for Min. She is not strategic in her communication and does not tailor her messages to the specific audience.

She knows this is an area of growth and wonders if Imani can be of any help. Min is still not sure about Imani's qualifications, and she is watching her closely. If Imani really did get the position because she knows someone and is not qualified, Min will not be able to rely on Imani for her own career development and support. The jury is still out on whether she can trust her.

Imani's Private Information

Imani has worked hard to get to where she is now. She is a product of a STEM initiative at her high school, and ever since then, she has been diligent in applying herself to get ahead in the technology field. She knows that, as an external hire for this new managerial position, she may not be favored by some within the organization. Naturally, people expect there to be more promotions from within the company to advance careers, and she wonders if there will be resignations as a result. That could be a negative reflection on her, and she's only just begun.

Imani is also sensitive about being a woman of color and worries she will be considered a diversity hire rather than someone who is intelligent and capable. She knows she needs to prove herself in these first months but doing so can be tricky. She wants to assert herself and demonstrate her worth, and at the same time, she doesn't want to come on too strong and be labeled in an unflattering and derogatory way. She's been in these situations before, and they cause her a great deal of angst.

She feels some tension with Min and suspects that Min applied for her position, but she's not sure. That is always a tricky situation, and she wonders why organizations do not do a better job at transitioning people in from outside the organization. She can see from just these first weeks that Min is very thorough and detail-oriented. She wants Min on her side because she can be a strategic asset.

Imani is aware that she is under a microscope and every move she makes is being examined, favorably she hopes. As the manager of the division, Imani feels it is her responsibility to develop good relationships with her team members. In this light, she wants to reach out to Min to build a good working relationship with her. She also recognizes her position of authority and is sensitive about not wanting any meeting she initiates to be considered a power play. She is not certain, but she feels Min is watching her every move very carefully.

Maybe she can set aside a time to discuss goals and see what Min's aspirations are going forward. As her manager, Imani is in a position to support Min's professional growth while getting the best Min has to offer to support the team and the division. Imani needs to be clear about the division's goals before this meeting, but she is still figuring it out. She doesn't want to be overbearing, yet she also doesn't want to appear clueless. She doesn't know how open and honest she can be with Min. Imani doesn't know how much influence Min has on others, and she doesn't know whether she can win her over, or if Min will be actively out to get her and conspire to see her fail.

Negotiation Preparation Stage

For Min and Imani to have a good working relationship, they will need to negotiate how they can work together effectively going forward. Part of their discussion should entail clearing the air. To do this well, there is preparation work they will need to undertake to glean the necessary insights and perspectives for an effective and successful negotiation. One part of this pertains to "self-work," in which each person identifies what is important to her. They both have made assumptions about the other and why they were selected or not selected for the managerial position. It will be helpful for both to uncover the source of some of the negative feelings they have toward each other.

As part of the negotiation preparation process, Min and Imani need to get into a mindset that will lead them toward a successful collaborative process. It is, therefore, important for them to adjust their mindsets so that they can put aside their negative feelings and frame this negotiation as the beginning of their relationship building (Figure 13.1). They cannot completely discard the assumptions they have made about each other because they do not have new information to replace those perceptions. One goal of this negotiation can be that they have an open mind and willingness to learn more about each other.

IMANI	MIN
Establish self as leader Earn trust of team members Provide professional development for team members Elevate profile of division in broader organization.	Establish technical competence Earn trust as reliable team member Gain professional development to advance career Build relationships outside of division.

FIGURE 13.1 Framing the Negotiation

Negotiations may be one-off events, or they may be a series of events leading to fulfilling long-term goals. By articulating their goals ahead of time, Imani and Min begin to see areas of interdependence. Chapter 9 explains more about framing goals.

They can focus on their interdependence in that they are both working in the same division for the same organization. Their success is interconnected, meaning that when one is successful, the other is more likely to be successful. They can also think about the ways they can be helpful to each other in fulfilling their goals. This can lead toward a more positive orientation and greater willingness to work toward win-win outcomes. They might entertain the question, "What can I do to help the other person be successful?" as a starting point.

Min and Imani need to think about what the other person needs while considering their current situation in the organization. Imani needs to establish her credibility in the organization, starting with the teams she supervises, and Min needs opportunities to continue to grow and develop her own career. These are not mutually exclusive: Imani and Min will both benefit if their team can be successful and if their individual contributions are highlighted when necessary. This framing emphasizes their interdependence and demonstrates that one person's success can fuel that of the other.

Another way of preparing for the negotiation is for each to frame how she thinks of herself as a negotiator. Min and Imani can each develop their own social and personal timelines of significant moments in their lives that shape the stories they tell themselves about who they are as negotiators.

Min

In Min's case, we can see from her social and personal timelines that there have been moments in her life when she had opportunities to speak publicly or present her ideas to others (Figure 13.2).

Min studied piano from an early age; her parents expected her to perform publicly, for her relatives, and later in

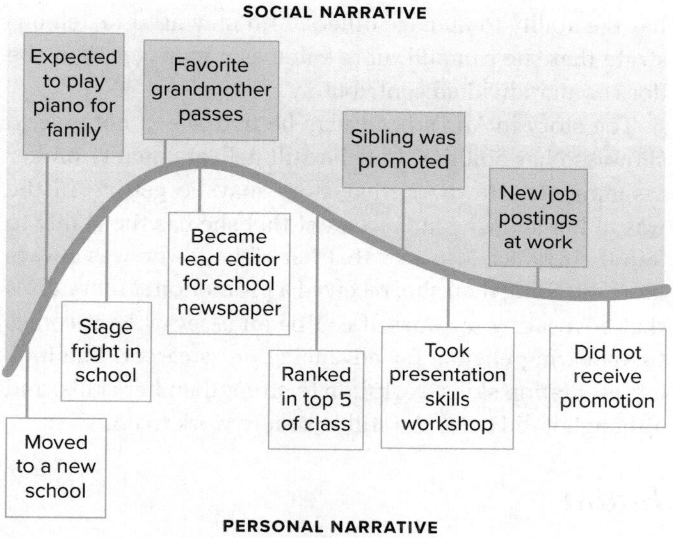

FIGURE 13.2 Min's Narrative Timelines

As explained in Chapter 9, narrative timelines capture key stories, personal and social, that may shape responses to current situations. *Adapted from the Serpentine Model used with permission by Cronen and Pearce in W. Barnett Pearce. Making Social Worlds:* A Communication Perspective *(Malden: Blackwell Publishing, 2007), pp. 154–56; permission conveyed through Copyright Clearance Center, Inc.*

school. Min was not comfortable performing for large audiences, even though she was an excellent piano player. She preferred to play by herself or for small, intimate audiences. Her parents wanted to showcase her achievements more, and Min felt obligated to follow her parents' wishes.

This orientation to avoid showcasing her talents and abilities followed Min into her adulthood. It is part of the reason she finds it so challenging to advocate for herself, and it may have been one of the factors that kept her from being promoted. It is well-known that Min is intelligent and a quick learner, but it might be a well-kept secret that she has the ability to manage others. Min may need to demonstrate that she can add more value as a manager than she does as an individual contributor.

The story in Min's head may be that she is not able to showcase her abilities, but she still delivers quality on her assignments. However, that story may be getting in the way of her showing management that she has the ability to join their ranks. Min sees that her sibling, who was always more outgoing than she, received a promotion. Min realizes that advocating for oneself can be an asset when it comes to appearing eligible for advancing one's career. She took a presentation skills workshop to strengthen her skills, and although it did help, she still has more work to do.

Imani

Imani's narrative timelines (Figure 13.3) show that early in her life she lived with her extended family and was well-supported. Then her family moved to an urban center, and she needed to change from a small, intimate, rural environment to a busy, crowded urban space with only her nuclear family as support. Imani was able to demonstrate her keen math skills in her new school and then benefit from a new STEM initiative for girls.

Imani did well in this space. However, she overheard comments made every now and again that she was benefitting from a focus on girls, especially girls of color, and later as a woman of color. This made her question her own competence and wonder about what she needed to do to prove that she earned these accolades and didn't receive them by default.

Remembering the feeling she had as a child of being supported by her extended family, Imani joined a support group for women of color in STEM. Being a member of the group helps her bring this feeling of being supported wher-

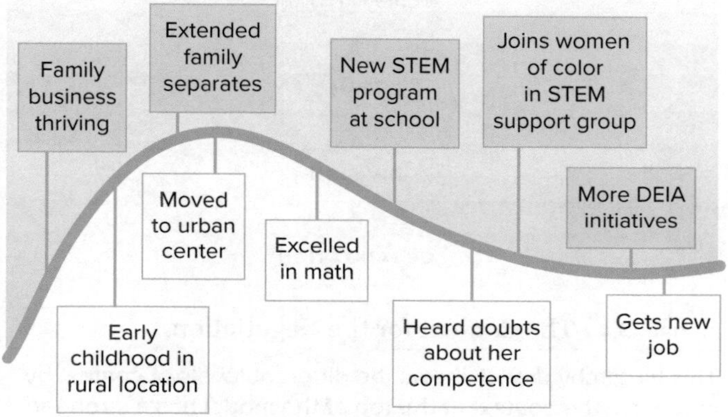

FIGURE 13.3 Imani's Narrative Timelines

Based on the Serpentine Model used with permission by Cronen and Pearce in W. Barnett Pearce. Making Social Worlds: A Communication Perspective *(Malden: Blackwell Publishing, 2007), pp. 154–56; permission conveyed through Copyright Clearance Center, Inc.*

ever she goes, and now in a new job she is looking to see how, where, and by whom she can be supported. She knows that success is a combination of her own efforts and abilities and having someone who looks out for her.

Min and Imani both carry stories in their heads about who they are as women, how they are competent, and what they need to be fulfilled and successful in the workplace. The awareness they gained by working through their narrative timelines surfaced what is important to them. Now, they can focus on what they need from each other and what their goals are for this negotiation and their working relationship.

Every negotiation takes place in a particular context, and the participants bring certain behaviors and mindsets, along

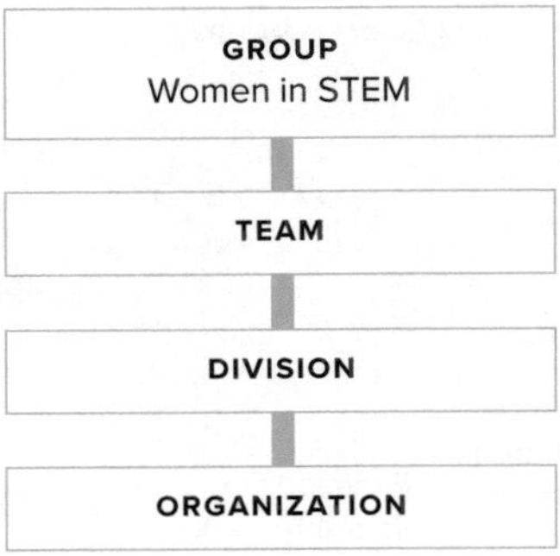

FIGURE 13.4 The Context for the Negotiation

This hierarchy model shows the different levels of context by category. The context at the top of the model has a stronger influence on mindset and behaviors than the levels below; the order can change over time. For Imani and Min, their shared STEM background creates a powerful shared context. *Based on the Hierarchy Model used with permission by Cronen and Pearce in W. Barnett Pearce,* Making Social Worlds: A Communication Perspective *(Malden: Blackwell Publishing, 2007), pp. 189–91; permission conveyed through Copyright Clearance Center, Inc.*

with the ways we "should" behave and what we "should" expect from others. This holds true for Imani and Min and what they expect of themselves and each other as they build their working relationship in the workplace (Figure 13.4).

Imani and Min are interdependent in that their goals are linked. When one of them does well, the other benefits. Imani's success as a manager can strengthen the performance of her teams, and Min will benefit. Min's success as an individual contributor increases her own visibility while contributing to the overall performance of the team and Imani's performance as a manager. Identifying common ground will enable them to name the overarching goals they can both work toward achieving that reinforces a positive interdependence.

In this depiction of the context model, we see that Min and Imani are both women in STEM. If they identify with this grouping, it will highlight their commonalities and have them collaborating toward advancing the state of women in STEM. There is also a camaraderie associated with that group and a mutual support that has been fostered over the years. Imani and Min will both benefit by supporting each other and strengthening other women.

Women in STEM should behave toward each other in ways that are supportive. Seeing themselves as members of the same group sets the precondition that they will be collaborative and supportive of one another. This being the highest level of the context model means that it has the strongest influence over the other contexts that fall beneath it.

They are both interested in helping the team succeed, and, as colleagues, they can work toward helping the team collaboratively because the overarching framing is that they are on the same team: women in STEM. This follows down all levels of the context model.

This is a fluid model in that the levels of context can shift. Initially, when Min was disappointed that she was not selected for the managerial position, that title may have been at the top of Min's hierarchy. Her subsequent framing of the negotiation and behavior would have been more strongly influenced by her wanting that position or not being selected for that position. It would have shaped her mindset and behavior differently in her interactions with Imani. Coming from the same group naturally fosters a more collaborative orientation.

There are both short-term and long-term goals in any negotiation. The short-term goals can be what we want from this particular negotiation. The long-term goals are how this next negotiation fits into a longer-term strategy made up of a series of negotiations (Figure 13.5).

	MIN	IMANI
Short-term goal	Build rapport with Imani	Build rapport with Min
Long-term goals	Build trust with Imani Establish Imani as a mentor and coach Advance her career with Imani's support	Build trust with Min Gain from Min's contributions to the team Provide constructive performance feedback to Min Exceed division performance with this team's support

FIGURE 13.5 Min's and Imani's Goals

Both Imani and Min want to build rapport in this initial negotiation so that long-term negotiations have a better chance of success.

In this case, Imani and Min have specific short-term goals to achieve. They both want to clear the air and set the tone for a more effective working relationship going forward. Min and Imani realize they have an interdependent working relationship, and they understand they have a need to establish rapport. This will foster more collaboration and will lead them toward meeting their longer-term goals. For Min, it is about continuing to excel in her performance and build her strengths to make her more eligible for future career opportunities. She wants to gain from Imani's experience and leadership even though she is still disappointed that she didn't get the promotion. For Imani, it is about hitting the ground running and performing well in her new position. She wants to garner Min's support to do this.

How they do it now needs to be determined. Min can seek guidance from Imani directly or by asking Imani to support her by sending her to workshops that develop her public speaking and presentation or managerial skills. Ima-

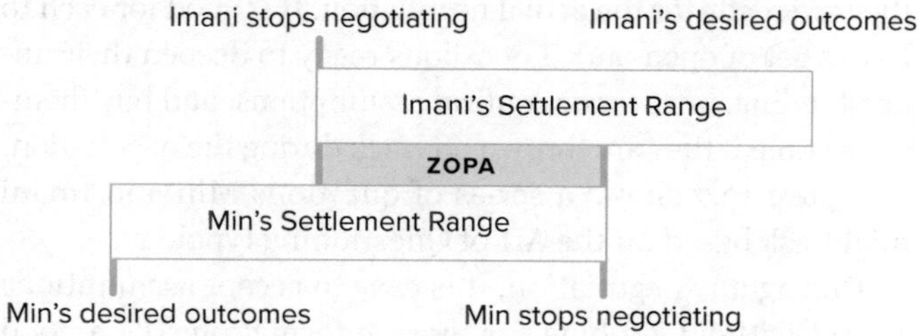

FIGURE 13.6 Imani and Min's Zone of Possible Agreement

In their preparation, Imani and Min clarify for themselves what they want, what they are willing to agree to, and those things they are not willing to compromise about. It is important to clarify so that there is a shared bargaining range that will allow them to walk away satisfied with the outcomes. *Adapted from Katie Shonk. "How to Find the ZOPA in Business Negotiations." Blog entry.*

ni can show her support for Min by giving her opportunities to shine. Doing so should increase Min's investment in the outcomes so she will want to be supportive and not block Imani's efforts.

All of this can happen because it takes place within a shared bargaining range. Min and Imani are clearer about what they want from each other and what they want to accomplish in this negotiation. Of course, in addition to their own preparation and negotiation skills, they are dependent on one another. Therefore, in preparation, they clarify for themselves what they want, what they are willing to agree to, and things which they are not willing to compromise (Figure 13.6). It is important to clarify so that there is a shared bargaining range that will allow both parties to walk away satisfied with the outcomes.

Negotiation Process Stage

Now that Min and Imani have completed their preparation,

they are ready for the actual negotiation. It is good for each to have a set of open-ended questions ready to deepen their understanding, uncover or confirm assumptions, and buy themselves time if they are thrown off track during the negotiation.

Figure 13.7 shows a series of questions Min and Imani might ask based on the Art of Questioning typology.

During any negotiation, it is easy to accept assumptions as fact without probing for more information. It's a good habit to slow down the pace and ask questions for more information. When the pace is too quick, we might skip over ambiguous comments and then build the rest of the interaction off of those assumptions. Slowing down gives us the time to question what we really know, the evidence we have to support those claims, and what else we need to find out to be more secure in what we have gleaned.

Min and Imani both have the goal of establishing rapport with one another so they can develop a better working relationship. Asking good questions of one another shows the intention of developing a better working relationship and a genuine interest in what each has to say. It also shows they are attentive and that each is invested in getting as accurate an understanding as possible. Asking open-ended questions buys time to regain emotional composure if one of them says something that upsets the other.

Of course, the tone and timing of these questions are also important. Min and Imani need to ask them with the spirit of true inquiry and curiosity, not as if one is grilling the other. It is also critical to let the other party finish what she is saying before interrupting with a question. Min and Imani will demonstrate more respect and gather more information by letting the other party tell the story the way she wants.

If either Min or Imani finds that during the negotiation she has lost control of the flow, and feels she is not able to address the issues she feels are important, there are a few tactics she can employ.

	MIN	IMANI
Clarification	It would be helpful if you could clarify what you mean by my contributions to the team.	Can you be more specific about what you are seeking in career advancement?
Probe Assumptions	In what ways have you observed that I have influence over the other team members?	What other scenarios can we assume might happen?
Probe Reasons and Evidence	What do you think are the reasons for this change in direction?	Do you have an example to help me understand better?
Viewpoints and Perspectives	Would you expand about your perspective so I can understand better?	What are some other points of view that might be helpful?
Probe Implications and Consequences	What happens if we do not meet our targets?	What are the possible consequences if that happens?
About the Question	I am not sure I understand what you mean by that question.	Please help me understand what is causing this confusion.

FIGURE 13.7 Communication Questions

There are many direct and indirect benefits of asking good questions. It can buy time, provide valuable information, and keep the negotiation flowing. These are examples of the kinds of questions that Imani and Min might consider.

The first step is to become aware that something is not going according to plan and to determine what it is. Here, it is critical to put to use the relaxation techniques they have practiced. This might include breathing, yoga, meditation, or visual or auditory imagery. Whatever they find useful that they can implement in the moment is helpful.

In any case, they will probably benefit from slowing and deepening their breathing. When we get tense or anxious, our breathing tends to become faster and shallower. They can ask an open-ended question to buy time. All of this slows down the pace and helps them realign to follow their preparation guidelines, if they are still relevant. They may need some adjusting along the way.

If there is still a need for more time, it is acceptable to call for a break. They can decide whether to resume after ten minutes or reschedule. They want to bring the best versions of who they are to the negotiation, and if delaying it for a while will enable them to regain their composure, that is better. However, in the case they cannot delay any longer, they will need to put these other practices into play to buy time in the moment to regain their composure.

Min and Imani can each do a scan of the different scenarios they planned during the preparation stage. They can realign as needed to follow the course of one of their scenarios. Alternatively, they may need to create a new scenario based on new information they received during the negotiation.

At different times during the negotiation, Min or Imani may suggest a new scenario. These what-if scenarios are part of the preparation process and may have been altered during the negotiation. There isn't a commitment on anyone's part; it is just a mutual exploration of what might happen. These could also be used to stimulate more collaboration if a what-if scenario was a worst-case scenario that could be shared as a warning between them to work it out during this negotiation.

For example, Min might propose the following: "What if you mentored me to strengthen my weaker performance areas so that I become more viable for a promotion?" Alternatively, Imani might propose: "What if you provided support to other team members in an area where you are strong, like creating mini training modules." Whichever scenario is proposed, Min and Imani will gather new information to proceed.

It is important to consider the timing of when these what-if scenarios are shared. It needs to be after a good amount of inquiry and sharing of information because Min and Imani do not want the other to think they worked it all out, are pushing their own agenda, and are not attuned and attentive to each other.

It is also a way to bring a taste of reality by grounding the negotiation and envisioning what could be in more tangible ways.

Post-Negotiation Stage

There are many exchanges in a negotiation. It is difficult to keep track of all agreements and the nuances accompanying them. Therefore, it is helpful to have some way of tracking the agreements in the post-negotiation stage.

This chart (Figure 13.8) is one suggestion of some of the criteria that Min and Imani can use to keep track of their agreements and next steps. This stage is especially critical when trying to change the tone of the relationship into a more trusting and collaborative one. Following up with this summary chart and perhaps an accompanying narrative will ensure they have the same understanding of what transpired. If there is a difference in memory about the agreements, it is better to sort it out directly after the negotiation rather than waiting until one or the other fails to carry out an agreed-on task.

It is also a chance for them to acknowledge that everything does not necessarily rest on their shoulders. By identifying resources needed, they can see who else they may need to call on for their support.

Through all this, Imani and Min will continue to build rapport with one another. They have several ways in which they can benefit from each other and have opportunities to further enhance their dynamics. They can do this by acting

ACTION STEPS	TIME FRAME	LEAD PERSON	RESOURCES	NEXT STEPS
1. Prepare goals	One week	Imani	HR—SMART goals	Share with Min
2.				
3.				

FIGURE 13.8 Follow-Up Summary

Following up with a summary chart and perhaps an accompanying narrative will ensure Imani and Min have the same understanding of what transpired.

on the things they agreed to in their negotiations. This will enable them to build trust and reliability, and will improve negotiations that will follow.

Reflection Questions

These questions appeared at the end of Chapter 4. The answers below pertain to the case study and may suggest how you could answer the questions for a negotiation you are about to have.

1. In what ways have you claimed value in your negotiations?
   a. Min claimed power by understanding her worth and her contributions to the team. She was able to ask for what she needed from Imani for her career development.
   b. Imani claimed power by asserting herself as the manager, initiating the negotiation, and aligning

Min's goals with that of advancing the team. The team's performance is linked to how Imani will be viewed as the new manager.

2. How do you claim your power in the workplace?
    a. Min is trying to develop more self-awareness. She wants to build on her strengths and figure out ways to improve in areas that may be holding her back. She knows her value to the team and she wants to use that to demonstrate her importance.
    b. Imani is finding ways to assert herself as the new manager. She has to gain the support of her direct reports, her peers, and her bosses. She needs to deliver, and by doing so she demonstrates her value add and confirms she was a good hire.
3. In what ways have you modified your mindset or behavior when it comes to your performance in the workplace?
    a. Min modified her mindset by moving past her resentment about not being selected for the managerial position. She is aware that she has some improvements to make, and she uses her working with Imani to improve herself.
    b. Imani does not want to use power over Min. She realizes Min is an asset and wants to build a good working relationship with her so that she can get the most out of Min, for Min's sake, the sake of the team, and for the sake of her own reputation.

14

Case Study 2: How Do We Take Care of Father?

This case study involves siblings who are faced with a situation that will be familiar to many of you. Negotiations among family members can easily become fraught, often with old stories clouding the present situation. But even longstanding issues can be resolved, or at least set aside, in the interests of finding a solution that works for all parties.

Shared Information

Sam and Sheila are siblings; they are negotiating care for their 68-year-old father, who has been showing signs of dementia. Their mother passed away three years ago from cancer, and since that time, they have been spending more time caring for their father. They've noticed that he seems confused at times—not remembering where items are located—or being unable to perform simple tasks, such as preparing meals. They are not sure how much of this is a new development since their mother did most of the household chores, or if he used to know how to do these things and now is unable to do so.

Sam and Sheila cannot agree on next steps forward. Sam wants to put his father in an assisted-living facility, so he can get 24 hour care and attention. He feels that his father's condition will continue to deteriorate, so they may as well put him into a facility while he is still able to acclimate to his new surroundings. Sam travels often for work, and he would have more peace of mind knowing his father is being taken care of by professionals. Sam does not have the time to be a caregiver for his father.

Sheila does not want to place her dad into a full-time facility because he is still mentally aware enough to live at home with part-time care. She feels that relocating him at this point will disorient him and accelerate the deterioration of his condition. He has already been through enough losing his wife—their mother—after 45 years of marriage. Sheila can rearrange her work schedule and care for her two children, ages nine and six, to help out with their dad.

Sam scheduled a meeting for Thursday with an assisted-living facility near Sheila's house in the suburbs. Sheila is annoyed that Sam made this appointment without consulting her, and now he expects her to visit the facility with him. She has to make arrangements for her children to be cared for after school since the timing conflicts with their regular pick-up time from school. She is willing to go along with Sam because she is concerned Sam will sign a contract for their father to move there, and she wants to prevent that from happening.

Sam feels Sheila is in denial and that it is inevitable that their dad will need this facility sooner rather than later. He knows it is hard to find a vacancy in a good facility and he wants to move ahead while there is still time, and while he is in the city before his next travel for work.

Sheila's Private information

Sheila is 37, three years older than Sam. She is married and has two children. She is more settled in her domestic routines and works part-time from home. She does not have a lot of time to devote to taking care of her dad, but she feels taking care of an aging parent is the right thing for children to do. After all, their parents were there for them their entire lives; it is the least they can do to reciprocate. Sheila lived at home during her university days and because her parents did not have the expense of an apartment, they bought her a car.

She realized she was fortunate to have one, as many of her friends did not.

In addition, their dad is still recovering from the loss of their mother. They were life partners, and Sheila thinks it important for their dad to remain in the house where he lived with their mother for 45 years. Her memory is alive for him in that house, and Sheila feels he would be disconnected from those memories if he moved to the assisted-living facility.

Sheila realizes Sam is more of a career person than she is, and she knows he travels for work frequently. It is hard for him to make the time to spend with their dad, or so he says. Sheila, however, feels that if Sam were to make visits with their father a priority, he would find the time. She thinks he is being selfish in not giving more time to tend to their dad. He is willing to pay for their dad's care, though, and that is a relief. Sheila works part-time, and her husband was recently out of work for eight months, putting them under financial pressure and constraints.

She feels conflicted about what to do with her dad. She believes he wants to stay at home because it is familiar and is the place where he spent time with their mother. She realizes eventually he will need to get more full-time care, but she doesn't want to give in just yet if she doesn't need to. She also does not like having a conflict with her brother. He is her only sibling, and they have been close over the years. He is also a great uncle to her children. One way or another, they need to find a resolution, and soon. She is planning to meet with him on Thursday, at the assisted-living facility. She has made arrangements for a friend to take care of the kids, so she will take advantage of her time with Sam and speak with him, maybe over drinks.

Sam's Private Information

Sam spends about 40-60 percent of his time traveling for work. He is eligible for a promotion to the rank of vice president in his company, and he knows his name is being tossed around for a VP position that is opening soon in a nearby state. Sam's career is important to him, and he wants to continue his trajectory to becoming a VP.

Recently, he has also been thinking about what is next for him in his personal life. He dates on and off but has not been involved in a long-term relationship. At 34, he feels he is getting ready for that in his life. He sees how full Sheila's life is with her husband and children, and while he may not want that exactly, he does want someone special in his life.

Sam has always looked up to his sister Sheila. She was there to support their mom in the later stages of her life and illness, something he found very difficult to do. He was always closer to his mom than his dad, and watching her deteriorate was too hard for him. Sheila seemed to have a better handle on the situation. Sam was glad to go to university away from home, so he could develop without being under his father's shadow. Now, however, he feels he is seeing the situation with his dad more clearly than Sheila, and he wants to take the lead in situating their dad in an assisted-living facility.

Sam does not see how he can make any more time in his life to provide caregiving for his dad, a request and expectation Sheila has placed on him. Sheila seems to feel that because he is single, he has more free time than she has. However, he feels she is not seeing or valuing the bigger picture of just how much sacrifice he has had to make to further his career. He does not criticize her stepping back from developing a career and choosing motherhood and family life. He thinks she should cut him some slack because they made different choices in their lives. She spends a lot more time at home and can, therefore, spend more time with their father.

Sam is willing to pay more than Sheila to move their father because he understands that he is better situated financially, especially due to the struggles Sheila and her husband are going through after his unemployment. While the financial commitment would have an impact on Sam's lifestyle and savings, it is a contribution he is willing to make. He cares about his sister and wants to ease her burden.

Negotiation Preparation Stage

To have a better chance of negotiating successfully, it is important for Sheila and Sam to prepare. There are many assumptions and old habits in their relationship that need to be uncovered and explored. In addition, it is important that Sheila and Sam address the main issue of their dad's care without getting sidetracked into old stories they carry about who they were as children and adolescents.

However, it is also understandable and maybe necessary for them to uncover these old stories and explore them together so they can change them and "mature" those stories to reflect more accurately who they are as adults today. If they are not in control of their emotions or how they want their stories to unfold, then the path will not be constructive. They will need certain skills to turn their negotiation into a constructive interaction. Preparation will ensure that they can do so.

In the preparation phase, there are several frameworks to use that will uncover information. There isn't a particular order for using the models, so we will go through a couple of the models here that Sheila and Sam could use in preparation for their negotiation with each other about their father's care. We can anticipate that this will be an emotional conversation because it is a sensitive topic to discuss the aging and deterioration of a parent. Added to that is any baggage they carry about their relationships in the family, including with each other.

As a start, let's look at the daisy models Sam and Sheila prepared in advance of their negotiation.

Below we can see the daisy model Sheila prepared (Figure 14.1). She placed in the center of the daisy the speech act that she will explore—taking care of their dad. On the petals around the center, she wrote down all of the factors that were important to her about this topic and that influence the stance she is taking. Sheila believes her father is still capable of living at home, and she feels it is important for him to do so to keep the memories of his wife, Sheila's mother, alive and well.

FIGURE 14.1 Sheila's Daisy Model

The Daisy Model, introduced in Chapter 3, is a way of visualizing the categories with which Sheila identifies in her decision making about how best to care for her father. *Based on the Daisy Model used with permission by Cronen and Pearce in W. Barnett Pearce from* Making Social Worlds: A Communication Perspective *(Malden: Blackwell Publishing, 2007), p. 180; permission conveyed through Copyright Clearance Center, Inc.*

We can see on the petals that Sheila has a very full life with her own family and part-time work. At the same time, she is very close to her dad, closer than she was to her mother. She wants him to remain at home because she is projecting that her dad also wants to remain in his home.

Sam also put "taking care of Dad" in the center of his daisy and noted the influences shaping his perspective on the petals (Figure 14.2). For Sam, taking care of his dad means being able to provide financially for his dad. Unlike Sheila, Sam was closer to his mom than to his dad.

Both siblings feel strongly that their opinion about their dad's future is the right one. The daisy models do not, how-

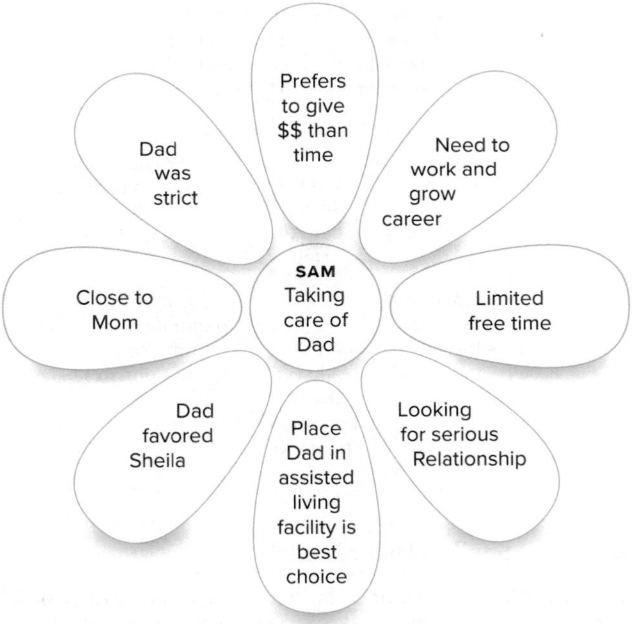

FIGURE 14.2 Sam's Daisy Model

Based on the Daisy Model used with permission by Cronen and Pearce in W. Barnett Pearce from Making Social Worlds: A Communication Perspective *(Malden: Blackwell Publishing, 2007), p. 180; permission conveyed through Copyright Clearance Center, Inc.*

ever, fully explore the stories they carry with them from childhood about their parents, themselves, and each other as children, and how they are now as siblings.

In the positions and needs chart (Figure 14.3), they explore their positional stances that describe where the conflict rests. Underneath the positions they are taking is the list of needs that inform their positions. There are several issues and concerns about not being recognized for who they are, what is important in their lives, and their contributions to the welfare of their dad. For example, Sheila feels she has always carried more responsibility as the older sister, and she wants to be given credit for all that she does in that role. She is also devoted to her dad and wants that to be acknowledged. Sam wants to be recognized for the adult he has become rather than being remembered by Sheila for who he was as an adolescent. He's built a successful, financially lucrative career, and he wants to be able to contribute to his father's care and be acknowledged for that contribution. He wants an equal seat at the table and to be recognized as someone who is able to carry some of the responsibility.

	SHEILA	SAM
Positions	Dad stays home	Dad goes to facility
Needs	Recognition for being a good daughter Being financially responsible Respect for being the older sister	Autonomy Recognition for building successful career Recognition of his financial contributions

FIGURE 14.3 Sam's and Sheila's Positions and Needs Charts

Sam and Sheila know they need to move away from their initial positions. They need to dig down to uncover and express their underlying needs so that they can find common ground.
Based loosely on William Ury and Roger Fisher, Getting to Yes: Negotiating Agreement Without Giving In *(New York: Penguin Books, 1981).*

There were two other exercises Sheila and Sam went through in preparation for their negotiation. The first is that each of them determined their best alternative to a negotiated agreement (BATNA). Here, they will get to see their other options, which will let them know how critical this negotiation is to them. If they have a strong BATNA, that means they have other good options. If they do not have a good BATNA, then this upcoming negotiation is very important. Figure 14.4 shows the results of that exercise.

Both have a strong BATNA. This means that if they step aside from their positional stance, they can see other options for satisfying their needs. Of course, this will take some recognition of these factors and a willingness to communicate and manage their emotions well during the negotiation. We can imagine that their relationship with one another is important, so there is hope they will be committed to the negotiation and work something out together.

SHEILA	SAM
1. If Dad has to go to a facility, visit often and bring him home to her house a few times per week.	1. Put Dad in a facility part-time if it can't be full-time.
2. Become Dad's caretaker at his house.	2. Hire a home caretaker for Dad to remain in his house.
3. Bring Dad to live with her and her family.	3. Defer to Sheila as the big sister and someone with more time on her hands.

FIGURE 14.4 Sam's and Sheila's BATNA Chart

Because they each prepared a BATNA chart before beginning their negotiation, they were able to find common ground.

Figure created by the author based on information from Deepak Malhotra. "Assess Your BATNA Using a Four-Step Process." In BATNA Basic: Boost Your Power at the Bargaining Table. *From "Accept or Reject? Sometimes the Hardest Part of Negotiation is Knowing When to Walk Away."* Negotiation *newsletter, August 2004, 3.*

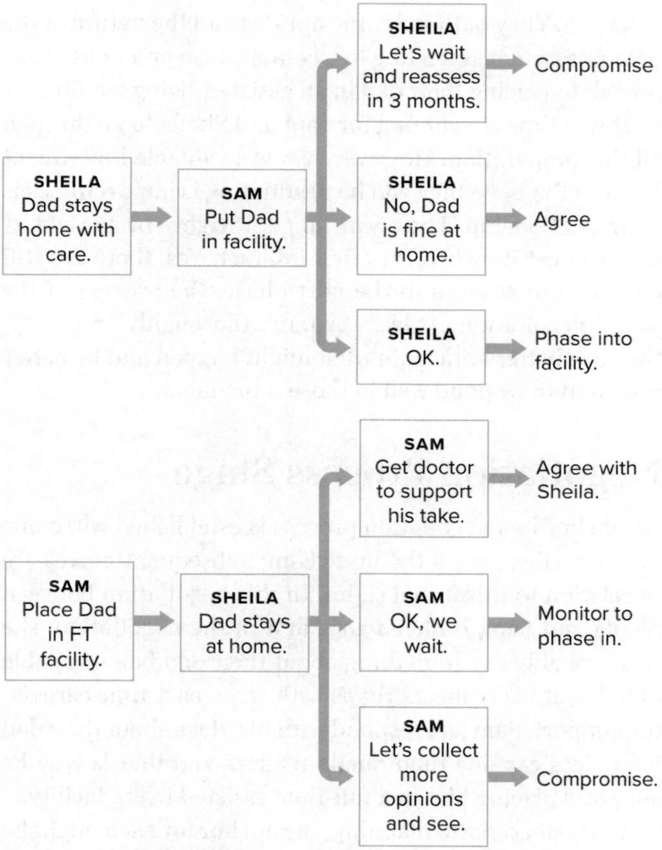

FIGURE 14.5 Sam's and Sheila's Scenario Planning

Sheila and Sam thought in advance about what the other's response might be so that they could each devise a way forward with the negotiation.

They also did scenario planning (Figure 14.5) so that they could anticipate what their sibling might say and envision the flow of the negotiation.

We can see here that Sam and Sheila both anticipated what will happen if their sibling stays positional as the first response. They outlined some options and the nature of the outcomes, such as leading to a compromise or a phased approach to placing their dad in an assisted-living facility.

It was time consuming for Sam and Sheila to go through all this preparation. However, it was a valuable investment because the issue they will be negotiating is important, as is their relationship. They want to get it right—or as right as they can get it—when they first interact. Yes, there are still emotions to address in the next phase, the process of the actual negotiation. At least by more thoroughly preparing, they can better anticipate what might happen and be better prepared to respond well in those moments.

Negotiation Process Stage

An anchor in a negotiation process is established when one of the parties makes the first claim; subsequent moves are in relation to this initial claim. In this negotiation between Sheila and Sam, if Sheila goes first in the negotiation, she will probably say something about their dad being capable of living at his home, perhaps with some part-time caregiving support. Sam will respond with his ideas about their dad being less capable than Sheila realizes and that is why he supports placing him in a full-time assisted living facility.

Without scenario planning, the anchor for each might be something like the following:

> Sheila: Dad is staying in his home and not going to a facility.
>
> Sam: Dad has deteriorated more than you realize, and he needs to go to an assisted-living facility now.

If they place their sibling relationship as the most important aspect of this negotiation, they might not claim those anchors and responses. Leaving the anchor and response as is could provoke a deeper impasse between the two siblings and lead to a more competitive negotiation. Instead, what they could do is lead with curiosity. This means they would ask each other questions to deepen their understanding of why they each feel the way they do.

The interaction could look something like this:

> Sheila: "Hi, Sam. You've mentioned that you think Dad is not capable of living at home and that he needs to be in a full-time assisted living facility. Could you tell me more about what you are seeing that leads you to that conclusion?"

Or Sam could lead with:

> Sam: "Hi, Sheila. You see Dad more often than I do, so when I saw him recently, I was shocked by how much he had deteriorated since the last time we visited. However, I know you think he is still capable of living at home with some caregiving support. Can you tell me more about what you've seen that leads you to that conclusion?"

The difference in this start to the negotiation is that Sheila and Sam appear to be open to hearing what their sibling has to say. They may still hold their own opinions even after hearing what the other person said. The difference is now they are more informed about each other's point of view, and each feels heard and acknowledged because they were asked to share how they formed their point of view.

Anchoring is important because it has a strong influence on the flow of the negotiation. However, there is also an opportunity to change the direction of the conversation in how the second party responds to the first party's anchor. For example, if Sheila started by saying their dad is fine and is staying at his house, Sam could follow with an acknowledgement of Sheila's opinion and then a query about why.

Sam: "I hear you, Sheila. You see Dad more often than I do, so when I saw him recently, I was shocked by how much he had deteriorated since my last visit with him. Can you tell me more about what you've seen that leads you to believe Dad is still competent to stay at home rather than move into a full-time facility?

Sheila may be defensive, but at least she is being asked to explain, and information will be uncovered. Sam is also acknowledging that Sheila spends more time with their dad and sees more of what he is capable of doing on a daily basis, whereas he does not see him often and can see the stark contrast in his condition. It gets the siblings talking and sharing information, which can lead them toward common ground and a shared understanding of the situation. This could also lead them to agreeing on next steps that will take both of their concerns into consideration.

In the case of unwanted repetitive patterns (URPs), Sam and Sheila could get caught up in unresolved sibling rivalry (Figure 14.6).

Sheila, as the elder sister, took on responsibilities that freed Sam to pursue his own goals. However, Sheila carries some resentment toward Sam because she thinks it is unfair. Sam doesn't like being criticized for being wild and irresponsible because he feels he has proven himself on many occasions but still wears that old label of being "wild."

If they stay in this negative looping pattern, they will not progress toward having a constructive relationship or negotiation. They need to become aware that they are carrying these old stories and then work toward modifying them. Sheila can say she is tired of carrying more than her share of responsibility and tell Sam how she would like him to contribute more. Sam can see if these ways make sense and then offer other ideas about sharing responsibility while reminding Sheila of ways he is already contributing. (Look back at Chapter 2 to see more about this topic.)

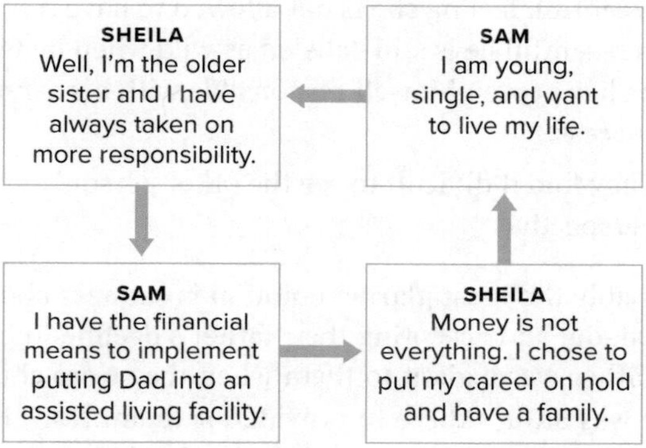

FIGURE 14.6 Sheila's and Sam's URPs

URPs are those destructive dynamics in relationships that block communication. In the case of Sheila and Sam, they are the old stories they told themselves since childhood. *Figure created by the author based on information from Vernon E. Cronen, W. Barnett Pearce, and Lonna M. Snavely. "A Theory of Rule-Structure and Types of Episode and a Study of Perceived Enmeshment in Undesired Repetitive Patterns ("URP's")."* In Communication Yearbook, *ed. Dan Nimmo, 232. New Brunswick: Transaction Press, 1979.*

All of these dynamics carry emotions with them. There are a couple of emotional triggers for Sheila and Sam that would bring them into a self-protective, defensive, and adversarial stance. If they can both be aware in advance about these triggers, they have a better chance of avoiding them during the negotiation. However, these emotional triggers may be caught up in unwanted repetitive patterns, and their pull can be very strong. These are some of the more obvious emotions that may surface in the negotiation between Sheila and Sam:

- Both siblings are hurting and finding it hard to accept their dad's decline into dementia.
- Because of their old stories of Sheila being the responsible one and Sam being the wild one, Sheila is

resentful, feeling she is not allowed to have fun; Sam is resentful he is still labeled as wild when he feels he has proven himself responsible with his career success.

- They find it difficult to see the other person's perspective.

Probably the most glaring emotion is sadness about acknowledging and accepting their father's decline in health. Their father was a giant to them when they were children, and he was always there to provide for them. Now, the tables are turning, and they need to care for their father; it is a lot for them to grasp.

Sheila, the older sister, and Sam, the younger brother, also carry stories about who they are as siblings. These stories are carried into adulthood, even if they no longer describe who they are as adults. Trying to change these stories but being pulled back into the childhood dynamics can also cause an emotional reaction. Sheila feels resentment that she carries an unfair share of the burden and does not have time in her life to be carefree and have fun. Sam carries resentment that no matter how successful and responsible he is in his professional career, Sheila still views him as the irresponsible and wild younger brother.

These old stories stir up emotions that can be present in their negotiations about their father. They are not directly related to the issue at hand—how to best care for their father—but they are present in the relational dynamics between the siblings. These emotions can interfere with addressing their father's care and distract their focus from the presenting issue. These dynamics and feelings of resentment make it hard for either Sheila or Sam to see the other person's perspective. They are stuck in their own emotional myopia.

Post-Negotiation Stage

Sheila and Sam were able to express their concerns and feelings about each other and their dad's situation. They decided after a long and emotional negotiation on the next steps to take. They are considering both their points of view. Some of the next steps include seeking more information, such as seeing other doctors to gather multiple opinions about their dad's mental status. This will help them be better informed when they do make a decision about whether their dad should stay at home or move to the assisted-living facility, or some combination of the two. They will also reserve a space in the facility for their dad because, regardless of when he is moved, it is inevitable that he will end up there one day.

It is important they write these steps down and frame them in a way they can both support. The language needs to be neutral so it doesn't trigger any feelings of blame or competitiveness. They covered so much ground in their negotiation that it is important to clarify exactly what they agreed to and not accidentally misrepresent a point that was not part of the agreement.

To move their sibling relationship forward, they need to recognize each other more fully as adults and all each has accomplished. Sheila needs to recognize all of Sam's accomplishments and acknowledge to him that he can be a partner to her in sharing responsibility. This will lighten her burden and allow her to spend some of her time on other endeavors. Sam needs to step up and claim some of the responsibility of caring for their father if this is what he says he can handle.

This negotiation is one that might have been overdue between Sheila and Sam to mature their relationship. The deteriorating health of their father forced the timing of it.

The issues they addressed not only pertained to making a decision about their dad, it involved the dynamics of their relationship as well.

Negotiations, especially among family members, can be layered and complex, with multiple issues that have become more complicated over time. It is a work in progress and, with improved skills and good intentions, family members can be motivated to improve the quality of their communication and relationships. This will probably not be the final negotiation between Sheila and Sam. Other issues will arise, and other family members will get involved. At least this is a beginning of developing better negotiation skills and represents a shift in the dynamics of their relationship. All of this will bode well for their future negotiations.

Reflection Questions

These questions appeared at the end of Chapter 5. The answers below pertain to the case study and may suggest how you could answer the questions for a negotiation you are about to have.

1. What are some of the stories you carry with you about who you are that started in your family?
   a. Sheila carried stories of being the serious and responsible one. This influenced her to always feel the need to take care of others, including Sam and her father.
   b. Sam was described as the wild one, implying he was irresponsible. He agrees that he was more reckless when he was younger and attributes that to being youthful.
2. In what ways have you modified one or more of these stories to better serve you?

   a. Sheila is learning through her negotiations with Sam that she doesn't need to assume all responsibility.
   b. Sam has a successful career and some really good ideas and insights about what to do for their dad. Sam can share responsibility.
   c. Sam is learning through his negotiations with Sheila that part of her take-charge attitude is not necessarily a reflection on him; rather it reflects the story she carries about herself. He has been changing his story to be a responsible professional and that carries over into his being a responsible son as well.
3. How have you generously modified the stories you have of others in your family?
   a. Sheila was skeptical at first but realizes that their dad is a shared responsibility, not hers alone. Plus, Sam is eager to be more involved and Sheila is enjoying the relief of sharing the burden. She is really pleased and proud of what Sam has accomplished and sorry she did not realize it sooner.
   b. Sam is realizing now that Sheila doesn't want to continue being the "bossy pants" of the family. She has been burdened by thinking she has to take on their dad, plus all of her family tasks. He is proud of all that she has accomplished and by how capable of a woman she really is.

15

Case Study 3: Should I Stay or Should I Go?

Healthy personal relationships often face challenges that require a calm, objective look at the situation and skillful negotiation to ensure that both parties are satisfied that they are being heard and their needs accommodated.

Shared Information

Eliza and Calvin have been dating for more than two years. Calvin, who works in finance, has just been offered an assignment in Brussels for one year with an option for a second-year renewal. His family lives in England, so this will be an opportunity for him to advance his career and be near his family after being away for nearly six years living in New York. He hopes Eliza will also be excited about this opportunity and go with him to Brussels. He sees a future with Eliza and is considering proposing marriage.

Eliza works in marketing and has been advancing her career at a quick pace. Her company is headquartered in Los Angeles, as they are US- and Asia-focused. Before the pandemic, she traveled to L.A. once a month to meet with the team there. She has been working remotely from her home in New Jersey since the pandemic. However, the company is considering reinstating the monthly team meetings in L.A. They are also thinking about having semi-annual or quarterly meetings in L.A. and at some of their locations in Asia, specifically Singapore, Bangkok, and Seoul.

Eliza wants to be available for these travel opportunities. She majored in East Asian history and literature at the university, and she sees the potential to continue growing her career with her current organization. However, she also cares deeply about Calvin and their relationship. She knows he wants her to travel with him to Brussels, but she doesn't want to leave her company and give up her career to move with him. Brussels to L.A. is a much longer and more costly trip to make once a month. She is reluctant to ask her company to pick up this added expense, and she also realizes that it is important for her to attend the L.A. meetings in person and not attend remotely, especially if others are together in the same room.

Calvin thinks it is possible for Eliza to be with him in Brussels and continue in her current job. If her organization doesn't value her enough to support her in this two-year period, he feels she should look for other possibilities. Brussels offers numerous opportunities: she has all of Europe at her fingertips and several Asia-centric companies work out of Brussels. Calvin is favorable toward an even longer stay in Europe than two years. He can see the two of them making a home in Europe, as there are many growth opportunities for them here. It doesn't have to be forever, but it could easily be for the next ten years or so. He hopes Eliza is open to this possibility too.

Private Information for Eliza

Eliza is happy for Calvin and this new career development. At the same time, she is also frustrated that it is taking him to Europe. Eliza likes Europe for its history and as a place for vacations, but not as a place to live. She is much more interested in living in Asia, maybe Singapore or Korea. After two years of dating, Eliza knows Calvin and she are at a critical moment in their relationship. She is not sure, but she suspects he might propose to her and that would make her really happy. Or it would have made her happy if he weren't considering this move to Europe.

Eliza is also at a pivotal moment in her career. She wants to be an important part of their growth plan. If truth be told, she hoped Calvin would want to pursue career opportunities in Asia. Singapore is a financial hub of its own, and she is sure there are chances for his success there. She knows Asia will take him farther away from his family in England and that he was excited about being closer to them by transferring to Europe. However, the growth opportunities for him in Asia are good.

Eliza is also aware of the choices some of her friends have made lately regarding their careers and starting families. After minoring in women's studies at university and staying current on the state of women in the workplace, she is annoyed that there are still so many binary choices. She wants to be able to have it all and not have to choose between career and family. Eliza remembers her mother being a stay-at-home mom until Eliza was in high school. She had a hard time re-entering the workforce and never really reached her career potential after so many years not working outside the home. Employers just don't value all the good skills you need to run a household.

Eliza feels that this next decision is not only about whether or not to go to Brussels with Calvin; it represents so much more for her. She doesn't want to be overly dramatic and say it affects the rest of her life, but it *does* affect the rest of her life. She knows Calvin cares deeply about her, but she doesn't think he gets how critical this is for her. She thinks Calvin has so many opportunities at his fingertips that whatever he decides to do he will land on his feet and thrive. She does not feel she has that same range of options.

If she goes to Brussels with Calvin, she feels she is giving up on her own dreams and that feels like defeat to her. She has not been sleeping well lately, and she is sure it's because of this tremendous decision weighing her down. She knows she needs to have a deeper conversation with Calvin to come to a better understanding of her feelings and the options they have available. She hopes she can keep it together and not break down and cry or become defiant. She needs to practice more of that calm breathing to stay in control of her emotions.

Private Information for Calvin

Calvin has been strategically positioning himself to be transferred to Europe as part of his career advancement. He is close to his family, and recently his dad's health has been failing. He wants to be able to spend more time with him, and being in Europe will facilitate that happening. It is too far from New York to the U.K. for frequent visits. He would not forgive himself if he squandered this opportunity.

All the stars seem to be aligning for him now—good promotion, exciting work, being in Europe near his family. The one downside is that it is not ideal for Eliza. He knows Eliza is committed to her current work situation and that she is Asia-focused. He thinks there are many more opportunities out there for her than she realizes. Her current job is not the only option.

Being in Brussels can also afford her possibilities of working with organizations that are Asia-focused. They would value her areas of expertise and her deep knowledge of Asian history and literature. She just needs to trust more and take a leap of faith that it will all work out. He knows she is anxious because she is watching what is happening to her friends and seeing that they are making choices about family versus career. He wants her to make up her own mind and not be swayed by what her friends are doing.

Calvin knows that there can be good opportunities for him in Asia as well. He is open to that as a possibility in the future. He just does not want to make that career move now because it will take him even further away from his family, and that is a deal breaker for him at this point. He wonders if Eliza knows the level of commitment he has to his family and how strongly that commitment motivates him to take this position in Brussels.

Calvin feels the pressure to make a decision very soon. There is a good deal involved in selecting and then preparing his New York replacement and getting up to speed on his new position. The head of the Brussels office is anxious for Calvin to get started and suggested Calvin come to Brussels for a week so they can begin planning. This would also involve finding an apartment.

Calvin wants to have a conversation with Eliza to explore this situation further before he commits to Brussels and goes there for a week. He needs to know she is open, and if she does agree to go, that she is doing it wholeheartedly and not reluctantly. If she doesn't have a good attitude about the move, it is not going to work. Calvin does not want to even consider that possibility.

Negotiation Preparation Stage

Calvin and Eliza are very invested in each other, their relationship, and their careers. It is important that they carefully consider how they communicate with each other, so that they can find common ground. Using the principles of coordinated management of meaning (CMM), we can see how *coordination*, *coherence*, and *mystery* are important to the foundation of their negotiations,

For Calvin and Eliza to *coordinate* meaning-making, they need to identify the ways in which their aspirations about their relationship and careers are mutual. They work in different industries with different titles and responsibilities, so they need to look beyond those differentiating details to an overarching goal they share. In terms of their relationship, they will need to be clear about what they mean to each other and their commitment to the relationship. The goal of this analysis is to allow them to be in sync with one another so they are a united force making decisions together.

Coherence, the second principle, is important for internal sensemaking. Eliza and Calvin both need to see the ways in which any move they make is aligned to developing their commitment to their relationship, as well as furthering their careers. Some of the connections and alignment are not obvious, and going through a process of making them explicit during a negotiation will assure their needs are addressed.

They can make their preparations and plan as much as possible, yet there are still so many unknown factors that are yet to unfold until after the move. This is where the third principle, *mystery*, comes into play. Eliza and Calvin can reassure each other through their thorough planning that they have set a good foundation and can weather whatever else comes their way. During their negotiations, they can explore different scenarios so that they are as prepared as possible for whatever emerges and know that they are in it together.

There are many stories that Calvin and Eliza carry about who they are, what they think about their careers, and what they think about the move to Brussels (Figure 15.1). Stories are created by our life events and our life events further develop the stories by which we live. Part of the negotiation preparation can include Calvin and Eliza both unpacking these complex stories they carry to be clear about what they know and what they still need to know to have a more collaborative negotiation.

It is important for both to make explicit these stories filled with emotions so they can better discern their underlying needs and what is of critical value to them, before engaging in a negotiation. The LUUUUTT, or storytelling,

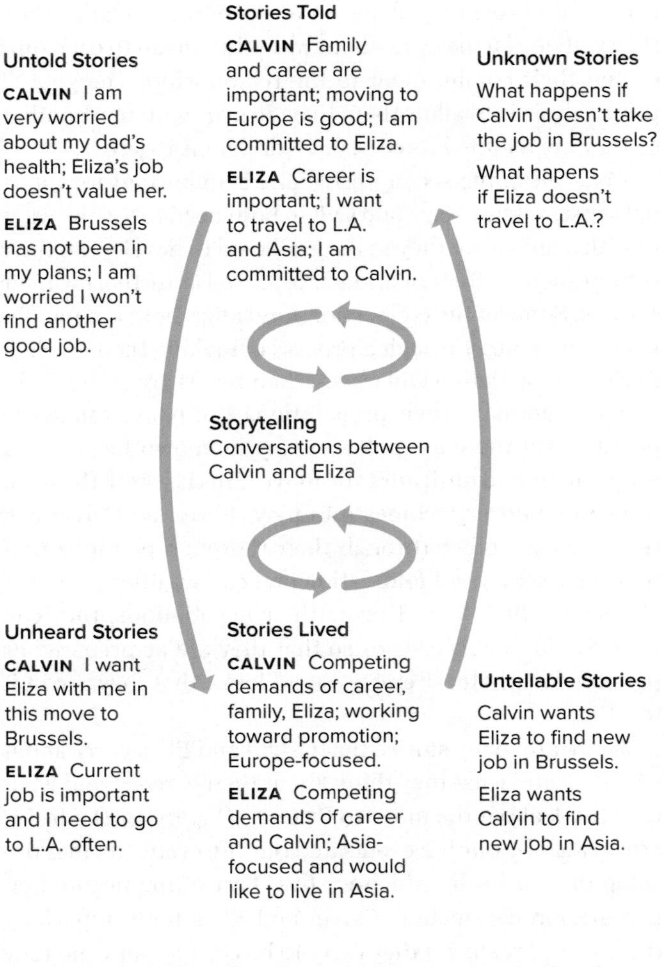

Stories Told
CALVIN Family and career are important; moving to Europe is good; I am committed to Eliza.
ELIZA Career is important; I want to travel to L.A. and Asia; I am committed to Calvin.
Untold Stories
CALVIN I am very worried about my dad's health; Eliza's job doesn't value her.
ELIZA Brussels has not been in my plans; I am worried I won't find another good job.
Unknown Stories
What happens if Calvin doesn't take the job in Brussels?
What hapens if Eliza doesn't travel to L.A.?
Storytelling
Conversations between Calvin and Eliza
Unheard Stories
CALVIN I want Eliza with me in this move to Brussels.
ELIZA Current job is important and I need to go to L.A. often.
Stories Lived
CALVIN Competing demands of career, family, Eliza; working toward promotion; Europe-focused.
ELIZA Competing demands of career and Calvin; Asia-focused and would like to live in Asia.
Untellable Stories
Calvin wants Eliza to find new job in Brussels.
Eliza wants Calvin to find new job in Asia.

FIGURE 15.1 The Storytelling Model for Eliza and Calvin

The LUUUUTT, or storytelling, model from CMM provides a useful template for surfacing these hidden stories. *Adapted from the LUUUUTT Model used with permission by Cronen and Pearce in W. Barnett Pearce, Making Social Worlds:* A Communication Perspective, *212-213. (Malden: Blackwell Publishing, 2007), pp. 212–13; permission conveyed through Copyright Clearance Center, Inc.*

model from CMM provides a useful template for surfacing these hidden stories.

Assume that Calvin and Eliza have each completed a model like this; this figure combines their stories and contains a great deal of information. One thing to look at is whether there are any gaps between the Stories Told and the Stories Lived. Most of the information is consistent in this case—a good thing because it indicates that Calvin and Eliza aren't deceiving each other, nor do they have competing demands. The main difference between the two is that, for both Calvin and Eliza, location is even more important than either of them is expressing. Calvin has a very strong commitment to Europe, and his commitment may be longer term than he is voicing. Eliza's commitment to Asia includes potentially living there one day, not just traveling there occasionally.

If they don't voice their feelings about their longer-term plans, each could appear to the other as being a bit stubborn. This possibility is further reinforced by the untellable stories in which they both want the other to relocate to the location they each want. Calvin really wants Eliza to find a new job in Brussels, further aligning their commitment to Brussels and being in Europe. Eliza wants Calvin to relocate to Asia with her, solidifying her desire for them to stay in Asia.

It will serve them both well to differentiate short-term goals and longer-term plans. Whatever they decide short-term, for the immediate future, they can schedule to revisit on a planned basis. This will reassure them that it is not fixed for life, because life events happen and may change their plans or intentions.

If the overarching goal is that they are committed to each other and making their relationship work, then it is clearer for them to see what decisions they need to make about what comes next. If they do not have the same level of commitment to their relationship, and other priorities are more important to one or both, that will also influence what they advocate for in their negotiation.

The approach they take to how they engage in their negotiation is critical because it sets the tone for the rest of their relationship and future negotiations. We can see the possible scenarios based on the five different approaches explored here:

- *Competing*: Calvin will insist on Brussels. Eliza will insist on staying in New York. Conflict will emerge from escalating emotions and ineffective communication.
- *Avoiding*: Neither addresses the issue at hand. Both are more stressed because decisions need to be made.
- *Accommodating*: One of them gives in to the other. Eliza goes to Brussels, giving up on her own career aspirations. Calvin doesn't go to Brussels or goes for only one year.
- *Compromising*: They identify what is most important and aim to satisfy those needs, letting go of other nice to have, but not critical needs.
- *Collaborating*: They engage in long, open conversations, figuring out a way to satisfy all of their needs.

If Calvin and Eliza take a competitive approach, it will be a win-lose scenario. One of them will lose and not feel good about it or their relationship. They may harbor a grudge, and it will not bode well for building an open, transparent, and trusting relationship.

If they avoid dealing with the main issues at hand, they will increase their stress and anxiety. A decision needs to be made because others external to the two of them are depending on hearing one way or the other what they have decided about going to Brussels. Calvin, especially, will feel mounting pressure to let his boss know his decision and that pressure will be transferred to Eliza too.

Accommodating might be a temporary fix, but one of them is not going to have his or her needs met. This may be satisfactory in the very short-term, but then denying themselves what they need will create mounting frustration that will eventually seep into their relationship. Either Calvin will resent Eliza for not going with him to Brussels, or Eliza might resent Calvin for taking her away from her current job.

Compromising might be a good approach as they explore the possibilities of their decision. They may not be able to get all that they want and need, but they might be able to get enough to make it work. There might be some short-term solutions that are satisfactory up to a point, with other needs being met at a future time. It is more of an agreement to delay satisfying certain needs rather than eliminating them all together.

Collaboration would be the ideal approach in that Calvin and Eliza can share all their feelings and concerns and work together to sort out what they need from each other and their careers in the short- and long-term. However, some situations have problems to solve and not dilemmas to manage, and they may need to compromise because they may not be able to work out all they need in the immediate solutions.

Negotiation Process Stage

During the negotiation, they want to put into effect all the good preparation work they did. What they do not want to do is go into a dynamic of looping in an unwanted repetitive pattern. They have been in a relationship for two years and in that time have developed some productive and unproductive ways of communicating and behaving with one another.

Figure 15.2 shows what a URP could look like.

Calvin is feeling pressured at work to inform his boss about his decision to transfer to Brussels. He does not want to confirm until he has a chance to more fully explore this move with Eliza. Eliza claims to be busy, and while Cavin believes her, the first one or two times she says it, he comes to feel she is avoiding the discussion. As more time passes, Calvin's frustration grows, and he increases the pressure on Eliza to have the conversation and make a decision. Of course, he wants her to agree to move to Brussels with him.

Eliza is feeling mounting pressure to make a decision about Brussels, and she is avoiding it by delaying the conversation with Calvin. She knows he has a hard deadline that is approaching quickly. However, she still has so many mixed feelings that she isn't ready to have a coherent conversation about it. The more she delays, the more frustration he feels, and the more pressure she feels, delaying the conversation even further.

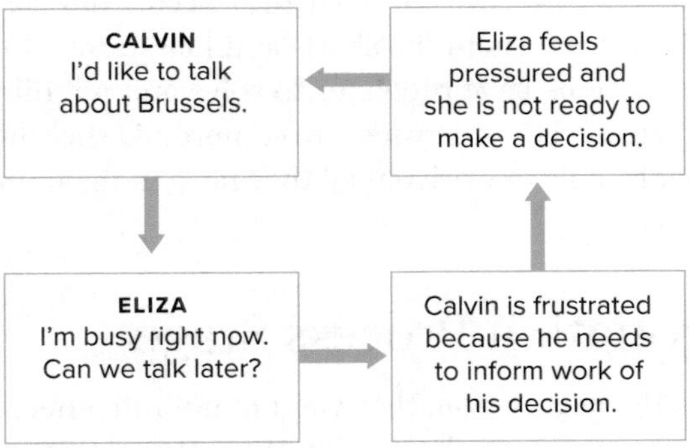

FIGURE 15.2 URP for Eliza and Calvin

Eliza and Calvin will need to refrain from engaging in unproductive communication patterns to ensure they have a successful negotiation. *Based on Patterns ("URP's")"* in Communication Yearbook, *ed. Dan Nimmo, 232. New Brunswick: Transaction Press, 1979.*

They need to break through this URP and have a conversation where they can both explore their many feelings and the logistics about what this move means to both of them. The negotiation is a good opportunity to share their feelings and concerns. In their preparation, they have each clarified what is important to them and decided they want to explore this opportunity in a collaborative manner.

In order to break an unhealthy pattern they have established, they each need to make a shift in their behavior. First, they need to recognize that they have this unhelpful pattern between them. Calvin needs to back down and have Eliza either initiate the conversation or set a time when she is willing to have this serious talk. Eliza needs to put a time limit on her avoidance and prepare herself for the difficult conversation. If they put their relationship and commitment to one another as the highest order of priority, chances are they will have the empathy, compassion, and patience to discuss this decision in a calm and collaborative manner.

This is a life-changing opportunity, which carries with it some excitement and some fear. They will both need to stay in control of their own emotions and the flow of the negotiation, including the pacing.

If Eliza and Calvin feel tense during this conversation, it will benefit them both to concentrate on their breathing. When stressed, we tend to have quicker, shorter breaths, and they need to take slower and deeper breaths to relax themselves. Bringing in more oxygen allows them to slow their heart rate and bring good oxygen to their brains. They are committed to each other and to having this conversation, but it is still a challenge because of the seriousness of the decision they need to make.

This is when it serves both well to have a practice they use to relax themselves. It can be listening to a certain song or type of music, visualizing a calming scene, doing yoga or meditation, and so on. They will not be able to engage fully in these activities during the negotiation, yet they can recall the calming effect these practices have on them. The more practiced they are, the more they will be able to imagine themselves engaging and triggering a calming effect.

They care about each other and their relationship, so staying focused on their compassion for each other will help to keep positive feelings. At the same time, they do not want to accommodate and only take care of the other party's needs, so they will need to stay firm in communicating and fulfilling their own needs. During their preparation, they probably envisioned possible scenarios, and calling on them now can offer guidance during the back and forth of the negotiation. Their relationship has a high order of importance, as does fulfilling their own needs. The preparation they did will aid them in staying on track and their relaxation practice will keep them calm and focused.

Post-Negotiation Stage

Following the negotiation, it is important they implement what they decided. There might be some follow-up tasks or additional information gathering. It is good for them to write up a summary, even if it is only bullet points:

What to do?

- Eliza could explore different remote work situations with her present company.
- Calvin could commit to looking into exploring options to work in Asia in three years.

Who will do it?

- Eliza and Calvin will both make efforts for more flexibility in their working situations.

When it will be completed?

- They will have immediate short-term conversations and longer-term commitments to continue the conversation about flexibility in working locations.

The action to be taken, who is to do it, and the date it will be completed can be as simple a summary as they need to prepare. Because of information-sharing and making of mini-decisions along the way, it is easy to have different memories of what was agreed.

In their situation, Eliza may explore with her current job how often she will need to be in L.A. or Asia and the extent to which her company will financially support her travel if she is in Brussels. Calvin may identify if there are options for him to work back and forth between Brussels and New York. He will still transfer to Brussels, but maybe he doesn't need to be there 100 percent of the time and can have some time in New York.

At least they will have listened to each other, heard the concerns of the other, and agreed to gather more information so they can more fully explore their options in making this work. Their perspective has shifted so that it is no longer a question of whether they will go to Brussels; rather they are agreeing that Calvin will take the transfer, and they are seeing the many ways in which they can make this work. It is a perspective shift that enables them to move away from a binary choice of go/don't go to a more collaborative approach of exploring the many options of how to make it work.

Reflection Questions

These questions appeared at the end of Chapter 6. The answers below pertain to the case study and may suggest how you could answer the questions for a negotiation you are about to have.

1. How have you become more conscious of what is important to you in your personal relationships?
    a. Calvin and Eliza agree their relationship is important. They also agree that their careers are important, and they are taking initiative in supporting each other in fulfilling their careers.
2. In what ways have you developed a better BATNA?
    a. Calvin and Eliza have shifted their BATNA from go/don't go to options of how to go to Brussels.
    b. They engaged in a collaborative negotiation, and they have a committed relationship, so they can comfortably share their BATNA with each other.
    c. They cooperatively engaged in brainstorming all different solutions and scenarios.
3. What strategies and tactics have you used to negotiate for what you want?
    a. Eliza and Calvin set a time to have this serious negotiation.
    b. They came prepared to have transparent communication, stay calm, and find a mutually beneficial solution.
    c. They prepared well so they could each understand what is important to the other and have a shared sense of what they could strive for during the negotiation.

Acknowledgments

The framing of this book is that negotiation is relational, and because of that, it is impossible to have written it alone. For that reason, there are several people I want to thank for being with me on this learning journey. I will not be able to name you all and for that I apologize. You are with me in spirit and know that you made a difference.

I am an observer of people—in real life, watching a movie, reading a book. I always wonder why people say what they say, why they made that choice of wording, and if it was even a conscious decision. I look to see if their intentions match up with the impact they have on others and if they are getting closer to or further away from their goal. Sometimes we need to get out of our own way. All that is somehow in this book.

Over the years, there have been so many colleagues, students, clients, and friends to thank for demonstrating good negotiation strategies, tactics, and skills. Some of you have challenged me to come up with more refined ways of framing negotiation, of drilling down to the essence of an interaction to get at the heart of what could be effective, what could create that behavioral and mindset shift. These layers of learning created what is in this book.

I want to specifically thank my family, who have continued to support me and keep me on my toes: my mother for teaching me the use of humor to get through even the stickiest situations; my daughters for teaching me early on that life is a negotiation and to choose wisely before committing to a course of action. They continue to excel and astound me.

My wonderful research assistants not only made my life easier but also unearthed nuggets of wisdom along the way: Lindsey A. Seiden, Kathleen Banzon, Gabriela Hutchings, and Jennifer Swann continue taking initiative and making a difference. Thanks to Columbia University for continuing to support me in my research and trusting me to direct the Master of Science in Negotiation and Conflict Resolution program.

Thank you to the wonderful team at Bold Story Press: Emily Barrosse for taking a chance on me, Nedah Rose for your brilliant edits, Julianna Scott Fein for keeping us on track, Laurie Entringer for a brilliant design, and everyone else who played a role in getting this book into and out of production.

A special thanks to all the women who continue to negotiate for what they need and what they want. My wish is that you stay uplifted and find the energy to persevere even if it doesn't seem like it is making a difference. Believe that it is.

Endnotes

Introduction

1. The Program on Negotiation (PON) at Harvard University, Massachusetts Institute of Technology, and Tufts University, continues to do research and practice on negotiation and has current trends in negotiation, as well as some historical or legacy information. Their website is: www.pon.harvard.edu.
2. Jessica A. Kennedy, and Laura J. Kray. "A Pawn in Someone Else's Game?: The Cognitive, Motivational, and Paradigmatic Barriers to Women's Excelling in Negotiation." *Research in Organizational Behavior,* 5, No. 35 (2015): 3–28.
3. Maria D'Agostino, Helisse Levine, and Meghna Sabharwal. "Gender in Negotiation: Preparing Public Administers for the 21st Century Workplace." *Journal of Public Affairs Education*, 6–7. https://doi.org/10.1080/15236803.2019.1579594.
4. There has been research on the role of implicit bias and how we are not even conscious of how we categorize and stereotype people according to the group affiliations we assign them. For more information on this topic, please see information on the Implicit Bias Test at implicit.harvard.edu. Another source of information on different types of biases is at the Perception Institute at www.perception.org.
5. For more information on How Stories Make Us Human, go to https://time.com/5043166/storytelling-evolution/
6. Henrik Kristensen and Tommy Gärling. "The Effects of Anchor Points and Reference Points on Negotiation Process and Outcome. *Organizational Behavior and Human Decision Processes*, 71, No. 1 (July 1997): 87. Article No. OB972713.
7. Two lists of top selling negotiation books include: https://www.amazon.com/Best-Sellers-Books-Business-Negotiating/zgbs/books/2686 and https://www.pon.harvard.edu/daily/negotiation-training-daily/negotiation-books-a-negotiation-reading-list/
8. https://www.payscale.com/data/gender-pay-gap retrieved July 14, 2021
9. Kimberlé Crenshaw at Columbia Law School coined the term "intersectionality" and continues to research and write on the topic.

https://www.law.columbia.edu/news/archive/kimberle-crenshaw-intersectionality-more-two-decades-later

10. For up-to-date research and information on brain imaging and how that helps us understand our brain functions better, look at https://www.nature.com/subjects/brain-imaging
11. Lutz Jäncke. "Sex/Gender Differences in Cognition, Neurophysiology, and Neuroanatomy," 87 (version 1; referees:3 approved) *F1000 Research* 2018, 7 (F1000 Faculty Rev):805. doi. 10, 12688/f1000research,13917.1
12. Two sources of information to learn more about the process of acculturation are: https://www.thoughtco.com/acculturation-definition-3026039 and The Sage Encyclopedia of Intercultural Competence at https://us.sagepub.com/en-us/nam/the-sage-encyclopedia-of-intercultural-competence/book238738.
13. Sayuri Hayakawa and Viorica Marian. "How Language Shapes the Brain." *Scientific American* April 30 2019: 6–9. https://blogs.scientificamerican.com/observations/how-language-shapes-the-brain/
14. Ibid.
15. Geert Hofstede, an anthropologist, led some of the groundbreaking research on cultural dimensions; one study is on culture's feminine and masculine traits. More information can be accessed at: https://hi.hofstede-insights.com/national-culture. Another source of information on how loose or tight a culture is, can be found at: https://behavioralscientist.org/tight-and-loose-cultures-a-conversation-with-michele-gelfand/
16. Geert Hofstede looks at levels of tolerance for ambiguity: https://hi.hofstede-insights.com/national-culture
17. Jordan A. Litman. "Relationships between measures of I- and D-type curiosity, ambiguity tolerance, and need for closure: An initial test of the wanting-liking model of information-seeking." *Journal of Personality and Individual Differences*, No. 48 (2010): 398. Elsevier.
18. Mitchell Hartman. "During the Pandemic, Women Are Less Likely to Ask for Raises and Promotion." *Marketplace Morning Report*. March 8, 2021. https://www.payscale.com/data/gender-pay-gap retrieved July 14, 2021.
19. David Poeppel, Karen Emmorey, Gregory Hickok, and Liina Pylkkänen. "Toward a New Neurobiology of Language." *The Journal of Neuroscience*, 32, No.41 (October 10, 2012):14125–31.
20. Lisa Feldman Barrett. *How Emotions Are Made: The Secret Life of the Brain*, 32. Boston: Houghton Mifflin Harcourt, 2017.
21. One of the writings that popularized social constructionism in 1967 by Berger and Luckman is a legacy source of information : https://www.amazon.com/Social-Construction-Reality-Sociology-Knowledge/dp/0385058985/

ref=sr_1_1?crid=9WOW5T87UPVQ&keywords=the+social+construction+of+reality&qid=1627222348&s=books&sprefix=the+social+construction+of+reality%2Caps%2C259&sr=1-1
22. W. Barnett Pearce. *Communication and the Human Condition*, 3. Carbondale: Southern Illinois University Press, 1989.
23. Lori Gottlieb. How Changing Your Story Can Change Your Life. Filmed September 2019 at TED@DuPont Video, 6:26. https://www.ted.com/talks/lori_gottlieb_how_changing_your_story_can_change_your_life/transcript?language=enrelations
24. The role of asserting one's own sense of agency can be explored further here: https://www.ncbi.nlm.nih.gov/pmc/articles/PMC5002400/
25. A core foundational book on basic negotiation processes and outcomes is the 1981 best seller, *Getting to Yes: Negotiating Agreement Without Giving In* by Roger Fisher and William L. Ury, published by Penguin. Its core outlook on hard, soft, and principled negotiations has had a major impact on the study of the field of negotiation.
26. Joel Pearson, Thomas Naselaris, Emily A. Holmes, and Stephen M. Kosslyn. "Mental Imagery: Functional Mechanisms and Clinical Applications." *Trends in Cognitive Sciences*, 19, No. 10 (October 2015): 599.
27. You can find more information on the psychology of fear and how it shows up in our brains: https://www.ncbi.nlm.nih.gov/pmc/articles/PMC3595162/
28. David A. Hogue. "Sometimes It Causes Me to Tremble: Fear, Faith, and the Human Brain." *Pastoral Psychology* 63 (2014): 659–71, 633. DOI 10.1007/s11-89-013-0593-x.
29. To explore the role of relationships in negotiation further, see the blog from the Program on Negotiation (PON) at Harvard, https://www.pon.harvard.edu/daily/negotiation-training-daily/negotiate-relationships/ Explore research done by cultural psychologist Michele Gelfand and her team at https://journals.aom.org/doi/10.5465/amr.2006.20208689

Chapter 1: The Stories We Tell

1. An interesting chapter on our narrative development across the lifespan is Kate C. McLean, "And the Story Evolves: The Development of Personal Narratives and Narrative Identity. In *Personality and Development Across the Lifespan*, ed. Julie Specht, 325–38. Elsevier, 2017.
2. Shelley Bird. "Sensemaking and Identity: The Interconnection of Storytelling and Networking in a Women's Group of a Large Corporation." *The Journal of Business Communication*, 44, No. 4 (2007):311–39, 348. doi:10.1177/0021943607306135.

3. Victoria Chen. "Transforming Power Through Systemic Questioning in Dialogue: A Perspective from the Theory of the Coordinated Management of Meaning (CMM)." In *The Coordinated Management of Meaning: A Festschrift in Honor of W. Barnett Pearce*, ed. Stephen W. Littlejohn and Sheila McNamee, 163–81. Lanham: Rowman & Littlefield, 2014.
4. Ibid., 175.
5. Ibid., 174.
6. Another type of questioning that is useful in uncovering assumptions and taking a different perspective is circular questioning, developed by the Milan Systemic Approach to Family Therapy. It is described in a book written by Luigi Boscolo, Gianfranco Cecchin, Lynn Hoffman, and Peggy Penn, https://psycnet.apa.org/record/1987-98650-000. A shorter paper summarizing the approach can be found in Jac Brown, "Circular Questioning An Introductory Guide." *A.N.Z.J. Family Therapy*, 18, No. 2 (1997): 109–14.
7. Victoria Chen. "Transforming Power Through Systemic Questioning in Dialogue," 173–4.
8. Brené Brown. *The Gifts of Imperfection: Let Go of Who You Think You're Supposed to Be and Embrace Who You Are*, 57. Center City: Hazelden Publishing, 2010.
9. For more information on the wonderfully accessible approach Brené Brown takes in talking about her research, please visit her website, https://psycnet.apa.org/record/1987-98650-000
10. Brené Brown, *The Gifts of Imperfection*, 57.
11. Catherine H. Tinsley, Sandra I. Cheldelin, Andrea Kupfer Schneider, and Emily T. Amanatullah. "Women at the Bargaining Table: Pitfalls and Prospects." *Negotiation Journal*. April 2009: 234. 10.1111/j.1571-9979.2009.00222.x
12. For more information on the social construction of gender, please review the research by Judith Lorber and Susan A. Farrell at https://psycnet.apa.org/record/1991-97120-000
13. Deborah Kolb. *Negotiating at Work: Turn Small Wins Into Big Gains*. San Francisco: Jossey-Bass, 2015.
14. Ibid., xxvii.
15. Ibid., 191.
16. Barbara Czarniawska. *Narratives in Social Science Research: Introducing Qualitative Methods*, 7. London: Sage Publications, 2004.
17. W. Barnett Pearce. *Making Social Worlds: A Communication Perspective*, 96. Malden: Blackwell Publishing, 2007.
18. For more information on meaning-making, visit the Coordinated Management of Meaning Institute (CMMI) website at www.cmminstitute.org.
19. Daniel J. Siegel. Mindsight: *The New Science of Personal Transfor-*

mation, 203. New York: Bantam Books, 2011.
20. Ibid., 204.
21. Hans-Georg Gadamer. *Truth and Method*, 281. London: Bloomsbury Academic, 2013.
22. I have written about the use of dialogue in conflict resolution processes. Beth Fisher-Yoshida, "Creating Constructive Communication Through Dialogue." In *The Handbook of Conflict Resolution: Theory and Practice*, eds. Peter T. Coleman, Morton Deutsch, and Eric C. Marcus, 877–97. San Francisco: Jossey-Bass, 2014.
23. For more information on dialogue, look at the works of Martin Buber, David Bohm, and William Isaacs.
24. Arthur Jensen. *A Call to Cosmopolitan Communication: A Narrative of Richness and Mystery*, 4–5. Oracle: CMM Institute Press, 2020.
25. Barbara Czarniawska. *Narratives in Social Science Research: Introducing Qualitative Methods*, 4. London: Sage Publications, 2004.
26. For more information on the work of Carol Dweck and a growth mindset, please visit https://www.mindsetworks.com/science/
27. Vernon E Cronen. "CMM, Argumentation, and Moral Force." In *The Coordinated Management of Meaning: A Festschrift in Honor of W. Barnett Pearce*, ed. Stephen W. Littlejohn and Sheila McNamee, 51–75. Lanham: Rowman & Littlefield , 2014; and W. Barnett Pearce. Making Social Worlds, ix.
28. For more information on CMM please visit the CMM Institute at www.cmminstitute.org
29. Morton Deutsch. "Cooperation, Competition, and Conflict." In *The Handbook of Conflict Resolution: Theory and Practice*, eds. Peter T. Coleman, Morton Deutsch, and Eric C. Marcus, 6–8. San Francisco: Jossey-Bass, 2014.
30. Morton Deutsch did research on this connection between process and outcomes in his *Crude Law of Social Relations*.

Chapter 2: How Words Affect Our Brains

1. Patrice Voss, Maryse E. Thomas, J. Miguel Cisneros-Franco, and Étienne de Villers-Sidani. "Dynamic Brains and the Changing Rules of Neuroplasticity: Implications for Learning and Recovery." *Frontiers in Psychology*, 8, No. 1657 (October 2017): 6. https://doi.org/10.3389/fpsyg.2017.01657
2. L. F. Abbott and Sacha B. Nelson. "Synaptic Plasticity: Taming the Beast." *Nature Neuroscience Supplement*, 3 (November 2000): 1178
3. More information on neuroplasticity can be found at https://www.verywellmind.com/what-is-brain-plasticity-2794886 and scientific journals, such as Neural Plasticity at https://www.hindawi.com/

journals/np/?utm_source=google&utm_medium=cpc&utm_campaign=HDW_MRKT_GBL_SUB_ADWO_PAI_DYNA_JOUR_X-&gclid=CjoKCQjwl_SHBhCQARIsAFIFRVVXOkV1poQ2toUB-Z6k6szp6ksrOVgs9sAlA3vEawUwiwmW8Bjz7QAkaAtTVEALw_wcB

4. For more information on memory and associations, please visit https://www.psychologistworld.com/memory/association
5. Sayuri Hayakawa and Viorica Marian. "How Language Shapes the Brain." *Scientific American*. April 30 2019. https://blogs.scientificamerican.com/observations/how-language-shapes-the-brain/
6. Tim Klein, Beth Kendall, and Theresa Tougas. "Changing Brains, Changing Lives: Researching the Lived Experience of Individuals Practicing Self-Directed Neuroplasticity," 21 (2019). Retrieved from Sophia, the St. Catherine University repository website: https://sophia.stkate.edu/ma_hhs/20.
7. Ibid, 10.
8. Lera Boroditsky. "How Language Shapes Thought." *Scientific American*, 65, No. 304(2): 62–5. Retrieved July 12, 2021, from http://www.jstor.org/stable/26002395.
9. Joyce Shaffer. "Neuroplasticity and Positive Psychology in Clinical Practice: A Review for Combined Benefits." *Psychology*, 3, No.12A (2012): 1110-1115. http://dx.doi.org/10.4236/psych.2012.312A164.
10. Klein et al., 28.
11. Peggy Holman, Tom Devane, and Steven Cady. *The Change Handbook: Group Methods for Shaping the Future*, 74–6. San Francisco: Berrett-Koehler Publishers, 2007.
12. For more information on appreciative inquiry, see the Appreciative Inquiry Commons, which is full of up- to-date resources, https://appreciativeinquiry.champlain.edu
13. Lisa Feldman Barrett. *How Emotions Are Made: The Secret Life of the Brain*, 1114–16. Boston: Houghton Mifflin Harcourt, 2017.
14. For more information on the role of visual imagery for both concrete and abstract information, please see https://www.oxfordhandbooks.com/view/10.1093/oxfordhb/9780199730018.001.0001/oxfordhb-9780199730018-e-008.
15. Voss et al., "Dynamic Brains."
16. For more information on breaking old habits and substituting new ones, please see Charles Duhigg's *The Power of Habit*.
17. For more information comparing the amount of energy the brain uses when performing habitual behaviors compared to doing something new, look at John J. Ratey's book, *Spark: The Revolutionary New Science of Exercise and the Brain*.

Chapter 3: Stories That Stick

1. Klein, Tim, Kendall, Beth, and Tougas, Theresa. "Changing Brains,

Changing Lives: Researching the Lived Experience of Individuals Practicing Self-Directed Neuroplasticity," 35 (2019). Retrieved from Sophia, the St. Catherine University repository website: https://sophia.stkate.edu/ma_hhs/20.
2. Ibid., 8.
3. For more information on identity development and identity crisis, please look at the work of the developmental psychologist, Erik Erikson, https://www.simplypsychology.org/Erik-Erikson.html
4. Donella H. Meadows. *Thinking in Systems: A Primer*, 11. White River Junction, VT: ChelseaGreen Publishing, 2008.
5. Ibid.
6. Ibid., 187.
7. For more information on systems, please visit https://onlinelibrary.wiley.com/doi/full/10.1002/sres.2215
8. Graeme S. Cumming and John Collier. "Change and Identity in Complex Systems." *Ecology and Society*, 10, no. 1 (2005): 5. Accessed July 19, 2021. http://www.jstor.org/stable/26267756.
9. Shelley Bird. "Sensemaking and Identity: The Interconnection of Storytelling and Networking in a Women's Group of a Large Corporation." *The Journal of Business Communication*, 44, No. 4 (2007):319. doi:10.1177/0021943607306135.
10. Sebastian Junger. *Tribe: On Homecoming and Belonging*, xvii. New York: Hachette Book Group, 2016.
11. Daniel J. Siegel. Mindsight: *The New Science of Personal Transformation*, 67. New York: Bantam Books, 2011.
12. For more information on us being social animals and having the need to belong, please see https://www.psychologytoday.com/us/blog/the-squeaky-wheel/202002/the-importance-belonging-tribe
13. Robyn Penman and Arthur Jensen. *Making Better Social Worlds: Inspirations from the Theory of the Coordinated Management of Meaning*, 15. Oracle: CMM Institute Press, 2019.
14. Bird, "Sensemaking and Identity," 317.
15. When we feel a part of a group we are in the "in-group," and when we are excluded, we are in the "out-group." We can be associated as in or out for different reasons; for more on this topic, please see the work of Henri Tajfel who coined *social identity theory*, https://www.simplypsychology.org/social-identity-theory.html
16. We pass through different rites of passage in the process of being acculturated into our societies. For more information on this topic, please see the work of Arnold van Gennep, *Rites of Passage*.
17. Shelley E. Taylor, Laura Cousino Klein, Brian P. Lewis, Tara L. Gruenewald, Regan A. R. Gurung and John A. Updegraff. "Biobehavioral Responses to Stress in Families: Tend-and-Befriend, Not Fight-or-Flight." *Psychological Review*, 107, No. 3 (2000): 411.
18. Ibid.

19. One useful tool to use to see the effects of holding on to our assumptions without clarifying them is the Ladder of Inference, https://www.mindtools.com/pages/article/newTMC_91.htm
20. W. Barnett Pearce. *Making Social Worlds: A Communication Perspective*, 178–80. Malden: Blackwell Publishing, 2007.
21. Meadows, *Thinking in Systems*, 16–7.

Chapter 4: Negotiating in the Workplace

1. Jessica A. Kennedy and Laura J. Kray. "A Pawn in Someone Else's Game?: The Cognitive, Motivational, and Paradigmatic Barriers to Women's Excelling in Negotiation." *Research in Organizational Behavior*, 35 (2015): 6.
2. Ibid.
3. Ibid., 7.
4. Much research is being done on the role of women in negotiation, especially in an organizational context. Some of the findings have been contradictory, but there are overall themes that have emerged and are addressed in this book. For more information on current research, please see the work of Deborah Kolb, Linda Putnam, Hannah Bowles-Riley, Catherine Tinsley, Emily Amanatullah, Julia Bear, and Andrea Kupfer Schneider, to name a few of the women researching this material.
5. Linda L. Putnam. Foreword to *Research Handbook on Gender and Negotiation*, ed. Mara Olekalns and Jessica A. Kennedy, viii–xviii. UK: Edward Elgar Publishing, 2020.
6. Interesting work on metaphors has been done, especially regarding how we think of organizations and our workplaces. One reference is *Images of Organizations* by Gareth Morgan and another is *Embodying Metaphors in Systems* by Sergej van Middendorp.
7. Henrik Agendal, Lars-Johan Åge, and Jens Eklinder-Frick. "Two Decades of Business Negotiation Research: An Overview and Suggestions for Future Studies." *Journal of Business & Industrial Marketing*, 32, No. (2017): 487–504.
8. Mara Olekalns and , Jessica A. Kennedy. "Spheres of Influence: Unpacking Gender Differences in Negotiation." In *Research Handbook on Gender and Negotiation*, ed. Mara Olekalns and Jessica A. Kennedy, 2–13. UK: Edward Elgar Publishing, 2020.
9. Robert K. Merton. "The Self-Fulfilling Prophecy Source." *The Antioch Review*, 74, No. 3, 75th Anniversary, Part I: Firsts, Famous, and Favorites, (Summer 2016): 504–21.
10. Another good place to consider the organizational metaphors Morgan examines is *Images of Organizations*.
11. Adam Maxwell Sparks, Daniel M. T. Fessler, Ashwini Ashokhumar, Kai Qin Chan, and Colin Holbrook. "Disgust as a Mechanism for Decision Making Under Risk: Illuminating Sex Differences and

Individual Risk-Taking Correlates of Disgust Propensity." *Emotion*,18, No. 7 (2018): 942–58.

12. For more information on measuring risk assessment in negotiation, please see Rodrigues, de Souza, and de Paula. "Negotiation Supported Through Risk Assessment."
13. Laura J. Kray, Jochen Reb, Adam D. Galinsky, and Leigh Thompson. "Stereotype Reactance at the Bargaining Table: The Effect of Stereotype Activation and Power on Claiming and Creating Value." *Personality and Social Psychology Bulletin*. PSPB, 30 No. 4 (April 2004): 405. doi: 10.1177/0146167203261884.
14. To read further in creating and claiming value in negotiation, please see Mehmet Bac, "On Creating and Claiming Value in Negotiations."
15. Deborah Kolb's and her colleagues' trailblazing work on women in the workplace and how to advocate for yourself is invaluable. Please see her many references from *Her Place at the Table*, 2004, to *Negotiating at Work*, 2015.
16. Catherine H. Tinsley, Sandra I. Cheldelin, Andrea Kupfer Schneider, and Emily T. Amanatullah, "Women at the Bargaining Table: Pitfalls and Prospects." *Negotiation Journal*, April 2009: 237. 10.1111/j.1571-9979.2009.00222.x
17. Adam D. Galinsky, Michael Schaerer, and Joe C. Magee. "The Four Horsemen at the Bargaining Table." *Journal of Business and Industrial Marketing*, 32, No.4: 606–11.
18. Much research has been done and much written about power and power dynamics, and from multiple disciplines, from organizational studies to critical theory and more. This has also branched into the work done on empowerment as well.
19. K. S. Cook. Exchange: Social. In I*nternational Encyclopedia of the Social & Behavioral Sciences*, (2001), 5042–48.
20. Ibid.
21. Morton Deutsch. "Cooperation, Competition, and Conflict." In *The Handbook of Conflict Resolution: Theory and Practice*, ed. Peter T. Coleman, Morton Deutsch, and Eric C. Marcus, 3–28. San Francisco: Jossey-Bass, 2014.
22. Andrea Caputo, Ayoko B Oluremi, Nii Amoo, and Charlott Menke. "The Relationship Between Cultural Values, Cultural Intelligence and Negotiation Styles." *Journal of Business Research* 99 (2019): 26.
23. Here is further framing on small "n" negotiations.

Chapter 5: Negotiating in Our Families: Family as a System

1. If you would like to read further on attachment theory, you can find more information at http://labs.psychology.illinois.edu/~rcfraley/attachment.htm

2. Jenny Brown. "Bowen Family Systems Theory and Practice: Illustration and Critique." *Australian New Zealand Journal of Family Therapy*, 20, No. 2 (1999): 94–103.
3. Marc-Charles Ingerson, Kristen Bell DeTienne, and Katie A. Liljenquist. "Beyond Instrumentalism: A Relational Approach to Negotiation." *Negotiation Journal*, 10.1111/neho.12078 (January 2015): 31–46.
4. Jenny Brown. "Bowen Family Systems," 95.
5. Ibid., 97; and Barbara Czarniawska. *Narratives in Social Science Research: Introducing Qualitative Methods*, 6. London: Sage Publications, 2004.
6. Much research on conflict resolution has been written up over the years. One good source of updated information is the Morton Deutsch International Center for Cooperation and Conflict Resolution (MD-ICCCR), www.icccr.tc.edu. Another source is the Advanced Consortium on Cooperation, Conflict and Complexity (AC4), ac4.earth.columbia.edu. Both are at Columbia University in the City of New York.
7. One type of family systems therapy that has influenced more recent developments in family systems therapy is Milan Systemic Family Therapy. A chapter by Pietro Barbetta explains it.
8. Lisa Feldman Barrett. *How Emotions Are Made: The Secret Life of the Brain*, ii. Boston: Houghton Mifflin Harcourt, 2017.
9. Ibid., 69.
10. Ibid., 72.
11. SMART goals have been popular for many years. This article talks about SMART goals and beyond. https://www.tandfonline.com/doi/abs/10.1080/09585176.2011.62721.
12. Feldman Barrett, *How Emotions Are Made*, 56.
13. Ibid., 657.
14. Ibid., 175.
15. Ibid, 32.
16. Emotional intelligence (EI) has been studied and written about over the years. Daniel Goleman is best known for bringing EI into the popular press.
17. Emily T. Amanatullah and Catherine H. Tinsley. "Ask and Ye Shall Receive? How Gender and Status Moderate Negotiation Success." *Negotiation and Conflict Management Research*, 6, No. 4 (2013): 253–72.

Chapter 6: Negotiating Personal Friendships and Romantic Relationships

1. One of the foundational books in the field that drew attention to interests and needs is William Ury and Roger Fisher, *Getting to Yes*. 1981, New York: Penguin Books, 1981.

2. Emily T. Amanatullah and Catherine H. Tinsley. "Ask and Ye Shall Receive? How Gender and Status Moderate Negotiation Success." *Negotiation and Conflict Management Research*, 6, No. 4 (2013): 253–72.
3. David Poeppel, Karen Emmorey, Gregory Hickok, and Liina Pylkkänen. "Toward a New Neurobiology of Language." *The Journal of Neuroscience*,. 32, No. 41(October 10, 2012):14125.
4. See the work of Brené Brown on vulnerability. www.brenebrown.com
5. William Ury. *Getting Past No: Negotiating in Difficult Situations*, 348–75. New York: Bantam Books, 1993.
6. Marc-Charles Ingerson, Kristen Bell DeTienne, and Katie A. Liljenquist. "Beyond Instrumentalism: A Relational Approach to Negotiation." *Negotiation Journal*, January 2015, 10.1111/neho.12078 (January 2015): 37.
7. Madison Long, William Verbeke, Tsachi Ein-Dor, and Pascal Vrtīcka. "A Functional Neuro-Anatomical Model of Human Attachment (NAMA): Insights from First- and Second-Person Social Neuroscience." *Cortex* 126 (2020): 282.
8. Lane Beckes, Hans Ijzerman, and Mattie Tops. "Toward a Radically Embodied Neuroscience of Attachment and Relationships." *Frontiers in Human Neuroscience*, 9, No. 266: 9. doi: 10.3389/fnhum.2015.00266.
9. Lisa Feldman Barrett. *How Emotions Are Made: The Secret Life of the Brain*, 139. Boston: Houghton Mifflin Harcourt, 2017.
10. Shelley E. Taylor, Laura Cousino Klein, Brian P. Lewis, Tara L. Gruenewald, Regan A. R. Gurung, and John A. Updegraff. "Biobehavioral Responses to Stress in Families: Tend-and-Befriend, Not Fight-or-Flight." *Psychological Review*. 107, No. 3 (2000): 413.
11. Daniel J. Siegel. *Mindsight: The New Science of Personal Transformation*, 204. New York: Bantam Books, 2011.
12. Amy Ingram, Whitney Oliver Peake, Wayne Stewart, and Warren Watson. "Emotional Intelligence and Venture Performance." *Journal of Small Business Management*, 573, No. 57: 781. doi: 10.1111/jsbm.12333.
13. Long, et al., "A Functional Neuro-Anatomical Model," 309.
14. Ibid., 310.
15. Ibid., 311.
16. Siegel, Mindsight, 60–3.

Chapter 7: Negotiating Outside of Work and Family

1. Rogers Brubaker and Frederick Cooper. "Beyond 'Identity." *Theory and Society*, 29: 1–47, 2000, 7.
2. Ibid., 4.
3. Ibid., 5.

4. Maya Zheltyakova, Maxim Kireev, Alexander Korotkov, and Svyatoslav Medvedev. "Neural Mechanisms of Deception in a Social Context: An fMRI Replication Study," 1. *Scientific Reports*, 10, No. 10713 (2020):1–12.
5. Ibid., 2.
6. It is an interesting phenomenon to look at whether you can trust and distrust at the same time. Roy Lewicki and his colleagues did some research on the subject and determined that yes, you can simultaneously trust and distrust.
7. Andrea Kupfer Schneider. "Negotiating While Female." Marquette University Law School Legal Studies Research Paper Series, Research paper No. 18–12, *SMU Law Review*, 70, no. 695 (2017): 694-719, 706–7.
8. Daniel Kahneman. *Thinking Fast and Slow*, 20–21. New York: Farrar, Straus and Giroux, 2011.
9. Decision making has been a popular topic of research, and much of it comes out of the area of behavioral economics, which is economics informed by psychology.
10. Rosa Li, David V. Smith, John A. Clithero, Vinod Venkatraman, R. McKell Carter, and Scott A. Huettel. "Reason's Enemy is Not Emotion: Engagement of Cognitive Control Networks Explains Biases in Gain/Loss framing." *Journal of Neuroscience*, 37, No. 13 (March 2017):3588–598.

Chapter 8: Negotiating Compromising Situations

1. Kelly Wallace. "After #MeToo, More Women Feeling Empowered." https://www.cnn.com/2017/12/27/health/sexual-harassment-women-empowerment/index.html
2. The #MeToo movement is still recent at the time of this writing. A recent research article by Ro'ee Levy and Martin Mattsson supports that there has been an uptick in the amount of reporting done after the #MeToo movement.
3. Adam Maxwell Sparks, Daniel M. T. Fessler, Ashwini Ashokhumar, Kai Qin Chan, and Colin Holbrook. "Disgust as a Mechanism for Decision Making Under Risk: Illuminating Sex Differences and Individual Risk-Taking Correlates of Disgust Propensity." *Emotion*, 18, No. 7 (2018): 951.
4. Ibid., 943.

Chapter 9: Lessons to Take with You: Negotiation Preparation

1. For more information on framing, please see the work by Linda Putnam, who has done a lot of research on issue framing.
2. Linda L. Putnam. Foreword. In *Research Handbook on Gender and Negotiation*, ed. Mara Olekalns and Jessica A. Kennedy, xv. UK: Edward Elgar Publishing, 2020.

3. Beth Fisher-Yoshida. "Transforming Intercultural Conflict Through the Context of Relationship." In T*he Sage Handbook of Conflict Communication*: Integrating Theory, Research, and Practice, 2nd Edition, ed. John G. Oetzel and Stella Ting-Toomey, 793. Thousand Oaks: Sage Publishing, 2012.
4. W. Barnett Pearce, Vernon E. Cronen, and Forrest Conklin. "On What to Look at When Analyzing Communication: A Hierarchical Model of Actor's Meanings." *Communication*, 4 (1979): 197.
5. For newer readings on CMM, please see Making Better Social Worlds: Inspirations from the *Theory of the Coordinated Management of Meaning and A Cosmopolitan Sensibility: Compelling Stories from a Communication Perspective*, both published by the CMMI Press at www.cmminstitute.org.
6. W. Barnett Pearce. Making Social Worlds: *A Communication Perspective*, 18–180. Malden: Blackwell Publishing, 2007.
7. For more on narrative transformation, see Beth Fisher-Yoshida. "Transforming Narratives for Conflict Transformation." In A *Cosmopolitan Sensibility: Compelling Stories from a Communication Perspective*, ed. Robyn Penman, 159-177. Oracle: CMM Institute Press, 2021.
8. There is a model in CMM known as the hierarchy model, which looks at contexts and the logical or moral forces within each context. For more information on the hierarchy model, please see W. Barnett Pearce, Vernon Cronen and Forrest Conklin's article "On What to Look at When Analyzing Communication: A Hierarchical Model of Actor's Meanings." There is also information on hierarchy models in Pearce's *Making Social Worlds* and Penman and Jensen's *Making Better Social Worlds*.
9. Jadranka Gvozdanović, and Katrien Maes. *Implicit Bias in Academia: A Challenge to the Meritocratic Principle and to Women's Careers—and What To Do About It*, 3. League of European Research Universities, 2018.
10. W. Barnett Pearce. Making Social Worlds: *A Communication Perspective*, 210–13. Malden: Blackwell Publishing, 2007.
11. Deepak Malhotra. "Assess Your BATNA Using a Four-Step Process." In *BATNA Basic: Boost Your Power at the Bargaining Table*. From "Accept or Reject? Sometimes the Hardest Part of Negotiation is Knowing When to Walk Away." *Negotiation* newsletter, August 2004, 3.
12. Katie Shonk. "How to Find the ZOPA in *Business Negotiations*." Blog entry June 28 2021, 1. Business Negotiations, Harvard Law School, Program on Negotiation, Daily Blog.
13. Dean G. Pruitt. "Strategic Choice in Negotiation." *American Behavioral Scientist*, 27, No. 2 (November/December 1983): 167.
14. Ibid.

Chapter 10: Lessons to Take With You: Negotiation Process

1. The book, *Humble Inquiry: The Gentle Art of Asking Instead of Telling*, by Edgar and Peter Schein, has a unique approach to improving communication and relationships through inquiry.
2. Frank Krueger and Andreas Meyer-Lindenberg. "Toward a Model of Interpersonal Trust Drawn from Neuroscience, Psychology, and Economics." *Trends in Neurosciences*, 42, No. 2 (February 2019): 93–4.
3. William Ury. *Getting Past No: Negotiating in Difficult Situations*. New York: Bantam Books, 1993.
4. Vernon E. Cronen, W. Barnett Pearce, and Lonna M. Snavely. "A Theory of Rule-Structure and Types of Episode and a Study of Perceived Enmeshment in Undesired Repetitive Patterns ("URP's")." In *Communication Yearbook*, ed. Dan Nimmo, 232. New Brunswick: Transaction Press, 1979.
5. More information on URPs can be found in *Making Social Worlds: A Communication Perspective and Making Better Social Worlds: Inspirations from the Theory of the Coordinated Management of Meaning*.
6. The use of an anchor can be further explored at pon.harvard.edu. Specifically, this is one of several articles on negotiation techniques, making the first move, and using an anchor, https://www.pon.harvard.edu/daily/dealmaking-daily/resolving-the-first-offer-dilemma-in-business-negotiations/

Chapter 11: Lessons to Take with You: Post Negotiation

1. More information on the value of following-up on negotiated agreements can be found at https://www.pon.harvard.edu/daily/negotiation-skills-daily/we-have-a-deal-now-what-do-we-do-three-negotiation-tips-on-implementing-your-negotiated-agreement/

Chapter 12: Going Forward

1. A classic in learning through reflection is Donald Schon's book, *The Reflective Practitioner*. New York: Basic Books, 1984.
2. Daniel J. Siegel. *Mindsight: The New Science of Personal Transformation*, 74-75. New York: Bantam Books, 2011,
3. Tali Sharot. *The Optimum Bias*. Cambridge: TED2012. https://www.ted.com/talks/tali_sharot_the_optimism_bias/transcript, 2:32–8:48.
4. Jessica A. Kennedy and Laura J. Kray. "A Pawn in Someone Else's Game?: The Cognitive, Motivational, and Paradigmatic Barriers to Women's Excelling in Negotiation." *Research in Organizational Behavior*. 35 (2015): 5.
5. Carol S. Dweck

6. Ibid.
7. Patrice Voss, Maryse E. Thomas, J. Miguel Cisneros-Franco, and de Étienne Villers-Sidani. "Dynamic Brains and the Changing Rules of Neuroplasticity: Implications for Learning and Recovery." *Frontiers in Psychology*, 8, No. 1657 (October 2017): 8. https://doi.org/10.3389/fpsyg.2017.01657
8. Jadranka Gvozdanović and Katrien Maes. *Implicit Bias in Academia: A Challenge to the Meritocratic Principle and to Women's Careers—And What To Do About It*, 3. League of European Research Universities, 2018.

References

Abbott, L. F. and Sacha B. Nelson. "Synaptic Plasticity: Taming the Beast." *Nature Neuroscience Supplement* 3 (November 2000): 1178–83.

Agendal, Henrik, Lars-Johan Åge, and Jens Eklinder-Frick. "Two Decades of Business Negotiation Research: An Overview and Suggestions for Future Studies." *Journal of Business & Industrial Marketing* 32/4 (2017): 487–504.

Amanatullah, Emily T. and Catherine H. Tinsley. "Ask and Ye Shall Receive? How Gender and Status Moderate Negotiation Success." *Negotiation and Conflict Management Research* 6, no. 4 (2013): 253–272, 2013.

———. "Punishing Female Negotiators for Asserting Too Much . . . or Not Enough: Exploring Why Advocacy Moderates Backlash Against Assertive Female Negotiators." *Organizational Behavior and Human Decision Processes* 120 (2013): 110–22.

Bac, Mehmet. "On Creating and Claiming Value in Negotiations." *Group Decision and Negotiation* 10 (2001): 237–51. https://doi.org/10.1023/A:1011210015279.

Barbetta, Pietro. "Milan Systemic Family Therapy." In *Encyclopedia of Couple and Family Therapy*, edited by Jay Lebow, Anthony Chambers, and Douglas Breunlin: 2–8. New York: Springer, 2019.

Beckes, Lane, Hans Ijzerman, and Mattie Tops. "Toward a Radically Embodied Neuroscience of Attachment and Relationships." *Frontiers in Human Neuroscience*, 9:266. doi: 10.3389/fnhum.2015.00266.

Bird, Shelley. "Sensemaking and Identity: The Interconnection of Storytelling and Networking in a Women's Group of a Large Corporation." *The Journal of Business Communication* 44, no.4 (2007): 311–39. doi:10.1177/0021943607306135.

Boroditsky, Lera. "How Language Shapes Thought." *Scientific American* 304, no.2: 62–65. Retrieved July 12, 2021. http://www.jstor.org/stable/26002395.

Brown, Brené. *The Gifts of Imperfection: Let Go of Who You Think You're Supposed to Be and Embrace Who You Are*. (Center City: Hazelden Publishing, 2010).

Brown, Jenny. "Bowen Family Systems Theory and Practice: Illustration and Critique." *Australian New Zealand Journal of Family Therapy* 20, no. 2 (1999): 94–103.

Brubaker, Rogers and Frederick Cooper, Frederick. "Beyond 'Identity.'" *Theory and Society* 29 (2000): 1–47.

Caputo, Andrea, Ayoko B. Oluremi, Nii Amoo, and Charlott Menke. "The Relationship Between Cultural Values, Cultural Intelligence and Negotiation Styles." *Journal of Business Research* 99 (2019): 23–36.

Chen, Victoria. "Transforming Power Through Systemic Questioning in Dialogue: A Perspective From the Theory of the Coordinated Management of Meaning (CMM)," in *The Coordinated Management of Meaning: A Festschrift in Honor of W. Barnett Pearce*, ed. Stephen W. Littlejohn and Sheila McNamee, 163-181. Lanham: Rowman & Littlefield, 2014.

Cook, K. S. "Exchange: Social." In Baites. *International Encyclopedia of the Social & Behavioral Sciences*. (Amsterdam: Elsevier, 2001): 5042–48.

Cronen, Vernon E. "CMM, Argumentation, and Moral Force," in *The Coordinated Management of Meaning: A Festschrift in Honor of W. Barnett Pearce*, ed. Stephen W. Littlejohn and Sheila McNamee, 51–75. Lanham: Rowman & Littlefield , 2014.

Cronen, Vernon, and W. Barnett Pearce. "Coordinated Management of Meaning," in *A First Look at Communication Theory*, ed. Em Griffin. New York: McGraw Hill, 1997.

Cronen, Vernon E., W. Barnett Pearce, and Lonna M. Snavely. "A Theory of Rule-Structure and Types of Episode and a Study of Perceived Enmeshment in Undesired Repetitive Patterns ("URP's")," in *Communication Yearbook*, ed. Dan Nimmo, 225–40. New Brunswick: Transaction Press, 1979.

Cumming, Graeme S., and John Collier. "Change and Identity in Complex Systems." *Ecology and Society* 10, no. 1 (2005). Accessed July 19, 2021. http://www.jstor.org/stable/26267756.

Czarniawska, Barbara. *Narratives in Social Science Research: Introducing Qualitative Methods* (London: Sage Publications, 2004).

D'Agostino, Maria, Helisse Levine, and Meghna Sabharwal. "Gender in Negotiation: Preparing Public Administers for the 21st Century Workplace." *Journal of Public Affairs Education*. https://doi.org/10.1080/15236803.2019.1579594.

Deutsch, Morton. "Cooperation and Competition," in *Conflict, Interdependence, and Justice: The Intellectual Legacy of Morton Deutsch*, ed. Peter T. Coleman, 23–40. New York: Springer, 2011.

Deutsch, Morton. "Cooperation, Competition, and Conflict" in *The Handbook of Conflict Resolution: Theory and Practice*, ed. Peter T. Coleman, Morton Deutsch, and Eric C. Marcus, 3–28. San Francisco: Jossey-Bass, 2014.

Duhigg, Charles. *The Power of Habit: Why We Do What We Do in Life and Business* (New York: Random House, 2014).

Dweck, Carol S. *Mindset the New Psychology of Success: How We Can Learn to Fulfill Our Potential* (New York: Ballantine Books, 2008).

Feldman Barrett, Lisa. *How Emotions Are Made: The Secret Life of the Brain* (Boston: Houghton Mifflin Harcourt, 2017).

Fisher-Yoshida, Beth. "Transforming Intercultural Conflict Through the Context of Relationship," in *The Sage Handbook of Conflict Communication: Integrating Theory, Research, and Practice*, 2nd ed., ed. John G. Oetzel and Stella Ting-Toomey, 791–813. Thousand Oaks: Sage Publishing, 2012.

———. "Creating Constructive Communication Through Dialogue," in *The Handbook of Conflict Resolution: Theory and Practice*, ed. Peter T. Coleman, Morton Deutsch, and Eric C. Marcus, 3–28. San Francisco: Jossey-Bass, 2014.

———. "Transforming Narratives for Conflict Transformation," in *A Cosmopolitan Sensibility: Compelling Stories from a Communication Perspective*, ed. Robyn Penman, 159–77. Oracle: CMM Institute Press, 2021.

Gadamer, Hans-Georg. *Truth and Method*. London: Bloomsbury Academic, 2013.

Galinsky, Adam D., Schaerer, Michael, and Magee, Joe C. "The Four Horsemen at the Bargaining Table." *Journal of Business and Industrial Marketing*. 32, no. 4: 606–11.

Gottlieb, Lori. How Changing Your Story Can Change Your Life. Filmed September 2019 at TED@DuPont Video, 6:26. https://www.ted.com/talks/lori_gottlieb_how_changing_your_story_can_change_your_life/transcript?language=enrelations

Gvozdanović, Jadranka, and Katrien Maes. *Implicit Bias in Academia: A Challenge to the Meritocratic Principle and to Women's Careers—And What To Do About It*. League of European Research Universities, 2018.

Hartman, Mitchell. "During the Pandemic, Women Are Less Likely to Ask for Raises and Promotion." *Marketplace Morning Report*. March 8, 2021.

Hayakawa, Sayuri and Viorica Marian. "How Language Shapes the Brain." *Scientific American*. April 30, 2019. https://blogs.scientificamerican.com/observations/how-language-shapes-the-brain/

Hogue, David A. "Sometimes It Causes Me to Tremble: Fear, Faith, and the Human Brain." *Pastoral Psychology* (2014) 63:659-671. doi: 10.1007/s11-89-013-0593-x.

Holman, Peggy, Tom Devane, and Steven Cady. *The Change Handbook: Group Methods for Shaping the Future*. San Francisco: Berrett-Koehler Publishers, 2007.

Ingerson, Marc-Charles, Kristen Bell DeTienne, and Katie A. Liljenquist. "Beyond Instrumentalism: A Relational Approach to Negotiation." *Negotiation Journal*, January 2015, 10.1111/neho.12078, 31–46.

Ingram, Amy, Whitney Oliver Peake, Wayne Stewart, and Warren Watson. "Emotional Intelligence and Venture Performance." *Journal of Small Business Management*, 57, no. 3: 780–800. doi: 10.1111/jsbm.12333.

Jäncke, Lutz. "Sex/Gender Differences in Cognition, Neurophysiology, and Neuroanatomy." (version 1; referees:3 approved) *F1000 Research*, 7 (2018) (F1000 Faculty Rev):805 (doi: 10, 12688/f1000research,13917.1).

Jensen, Arthur. *A Call to Cosmopolitan Communication: A Narrative of Richness and Mystery*. Oracle: CMM Institute Press, 2020.

Junger, Sebastian. *Tribe: On Homecoming and Belonging*. New York: Hachette Book Group, 2016.

Kahneman, Daniel. *Thinking Fast and Slow*. New York: Farrar, Straus and Giroux, 2011.

Kennedy, Jessica A. and Laura J. Kray. "A Pawn in Someone Else's Game? The Cognitive, Motivational, and Paradigmatic Barriers to Women's Excelling in Negotiation." *Research in Organizational Behavior*, 35 (2015): 3–28.

Klein, Tim, Beth Kendall, and Theresa Tougas. "Changing Brains, Changing Lives: Researching the Lived Experience of Individuals Practicing Self-Directed Neuroplasticity." 2019. Retrieved from Sophia, the St. Catherine University repository website: https://sophia.stkate.edu/ma_hhs/20.

Kolb, Deborah. *Negotiating at Work: Turn Small Wins into Big Gains*. San Francisco: Jossey-Bass, 2015.

Kolb, Deborah M., Judith Williams, and Carol Frohlinger. *Her Place at the Table: A Woman's Guide to Negotiating Five Key Challenges to Leadership Success*. San Francisco: Jossey-Bass, 2004.

Kraus, Wolfgang. "The Narrative Negotiation of Identity and Belonging." *Narrative Inquiry*, 16, no. 1 (2006): 103–11.

Kray, Laura J., Jochen Reb, Adam D. Galinsky, and Leigh Thompson. "Stereotype Reactance at the Bargaining Table: The Effect of Stereotype Activation and Power on Claiming and Creating Value." *Personality and Social Psychology Bulletin*,vol. 30, no. 4 (April 2004): 399–411. doi: 10.1177/0146167203261884.

Kristensen, Henrik and Tommy Gärling. "The Effects of Anchor Points and Reference Points on Negotiation Process and Outcome." *Organizational Behavior and Human Decision Processes*, 71, no.1 (July 1997): 85–94. Article No. OB972713.

Krueger, Frank, and Andreas Meyer-Lindenberg. "Toward a Model of Interpersonal Trust Drawn From Neuroscience, Psychology, and Economics." *Trends in Neurosciences*, 42, No. 2 (February 2019).

Kupfer Schneider, Andrea. "Negotiating While Female." Marquette University Law School Legal Studies Research Paper Series, Research paper No. 18-12, *SMU Law Review* 70 (2017): 694–719.

Levy, Roee, and Martin Mattsson. "The Effects of Social Movements: Evidence from #MeToo," July 22, 2020. Available at SSRN: https://ssrn.com/abstract=3496903 or http://dx.doi.org/10.2139/ssrn.3496903

Lewicki, Roy J., Daniel J. McAllister, and Robert J. Bies. "Trust and Distrust: New Relationships and Realities." *Academy of Management Review*, 23, No. 3 (1 July 1998). https://doi.org/10.5465/amr.1998.926620

Li, Rosa, David V. Smith, John A. Clithero, Vinod Venkatraman, Vinod, R. McKell Carter, and Scott A. Huettel, "Reason's Enemy is Not Emotion: Engagement of Cognitive Control Networks Explains Biases in Gain/Loss Framing." *Journal of Neuroscience*, 37, No. 13 (March 2017):3588–98.

Libby, Lisa K. and Richard P. Eibach. "The Role of Visual Imagery on Social Cognition." In T*he Oxford Handbook of Social Cognition*, ed. Donal Carlston, 147-166. Oxford: Oxford University Press.

Litman, Jordan A. "Relationships between measures of I- and D-type curiosity, ambiguity tolerance, and need for closure: An initial test of the wanting-liking model of information-seeking." *Journal of Personality and Individual Differences*, 48 (2010): 397–402. Elsevier.

Long, Madison, Willem Verbeke, Tsachi Ein-Dor, and Pascal Vrtīcka. "A Functional Neuro-Anatomical Model of Human Attachment (NAMA): Insights from First- and Second-Person Social Neuroscience." *Cortex* 126 (2020): 281–321.

Malhotra, Deepak. "Assess Your BATNA Using a Four-Step Process." In *BATNA Basic: Boost Your Power at the Bargaining Table*. From "Accept or Reject? Sometimes the Hardest Part of Negotiation is Knowing When to Walk Away." *Negotiation* newsletter, August 2004.

McAdams, Dan P. "The psychological self as actor, agent, and author." *Perspectives on Psychological Science*, 8: 272–95. https://doi.org/10.1177/1745691612464657

Meadows, Donella H. *Thinking in Systems: A Primer*. White River Junction, VT: Chelsea Green Publishing, 2008.

Merton, Robert K. "The Self-Fulfilling Prophecy Source." *The Antioch Review*, 74, No. 3, 75th Anniversary, Part I: Firsts, Famous, and Favorites, (Summer 2016): 504–21.

Morgan, Gareth. *Images of Organizations*. Thousand Oaks: Sage Publishers, 2006.

Olekalns, Mara and Jessica A. Kennedy. "Spheres of Influence: Unpacking Gender Differences In Negotiation." In *Research Handbook on Gender and Negotiation*, ed. Mara Olekalns and Jessica A. Kennedy, 2–13. UK: Edward Elgar Publishing, 2020. https://www.payscale.com/data/gender-pay-gap retrieved July 14, 2021

Pearce, W. Barnett. *Communication and the Human Condition*. Carbondale: Southern Illinois University Press, 1998.

———. *Making Social Worlds: A Communication Perspective*. Malden: Blackwell Publishing, 2007.

———., Vernon E. Cronen, and Forrest, Conklin. "On What to Look at When Analyzing Communication: A Hierarchical Model of Actor's Meanings." *Communication*, 4 (1979): 195–220.

Pearson, Joel, Thomas Naselaris, Emily A. Holmes, and Stephen M. Kosslyn. "Mental Imagery: Functional Mechanisms and Clinical Applications." *Trends in Cognitive Sciences*, 19, No. 10 (October 2015): 590–602.

Penman, Robyn (Ed.). *A Cosmopolitan Sensibility: Compelling Stories from a Communication Perspective*. Oracle: CMM Institute Press, 2021.

———, and Arthur Jensen. *Making Better Social Worlds: Inspirations from the Theory of the Coordinated Management of Meaning*. Oracle: CMM Institute Press, 2019.

Poeppel, David, Karen Emmorey, Gregory Hickok, and Liina Pylkkänen. "Toward a New Neurobiology of Language." *The Journal of Neuroscience*, 32, No. 41(October 10, 2012):14125–31.

Pruitt, Dean G. "Strategic Choice in Negotiation." *American Behavioral Scientist*, 27, No. 2 (November/December 1983): 167–94.

Putnam, Linda L. Foreword to *Research Handbook on Gender and Negotiation*, ed. Mara Olekalns and Jessica A. Kennedy, viii-xviii. UK: Edward Elgar Publishing, 2020.

Putnam, Linda L., and Majia Holmer. "Framing, Reframing, and Issue Development." In *Communication and Negotiation*, ed. Linda L. Putnam and Michael E. Roloff, 128–155. Thousand Oaks: Sage Publications, 1992.

Ratey, John J. Spark: *The Revolutionary New Science of Exercise and the Brain*. New York: Little and Brown, 2008.

Rodrigues, Sérgio Assis, Jano de Souza, and Melise de Paula. "Negotiation Supported Through Risk Assessment." In the *Proceedings of the Tenth International Conference on Enterprise Information Systems, AIDSS* (2008): 488–91.

Schein, Edgar H. and Peter A. Schein. *Humble Inquiry: The Gentle Art of Asking Instead of Telling*. San Francisco: Berrett-Koehler, 2021.

Schon, Donald A. *The Reflective Practitioner: How Professionals Think in Action*. New York: Basic Books, 1984.

Shaffer, Joyce. "Neuroplasticity and Positive Psychology in Clinical Practice: A Review for Combined Benefits." *Psychology*, 3, No.12A (2012): 1110–1115. http://dx.doi.org/10.4236/psych.2012.312A164.

Sharot, Tali. *The Optimum Bias*. Cambridge: TED2012. https://www.ted.com/talks/tali_sharot_the_optimism_bias/transcript

Shonk, Katie. "How to Find the ZOPA in Business Negotiations." Blog entry June 28 2021. Business Negotiations, Harvard Law School, Program on Negotiation, Daily Blog. https://www.pon.harvard.edu/daily/business-negotiations/how-to-find-the-zopa-in-business-negotiations/.

Siegel, Daniel J. Mindsight: *The New Science of Personal Transformation*. New York: Bantam Books, 2011.

Sparks, Adam Maxwell, Daniel M. T. Fessler, Ashwini Ashokhumar, Chan Kai Qin, and Colin Holbrook. "Disgust as a Mechanism for Decision Making Under Risk: Illuminating Sex Differences and Individual Risk-Taking Correlates of Disgust Propensity." *Emotion*, 18, No. 7 (2018): 942–58.

Taylor, Shelley E., Laura Cousino Klein, Brian P. Lewis, Tara L. Gruenewald, Regan A. R. Gurung, and John A. Updegraff, John A. "Biobehavioral Responses to Stress in Families: Tend-and-Befriend, Not Fight-or-Flight." *Psychological Review*, 107, No. 3 (2000): 411–29.

Tinsley, Catherine H., Sandra I. Cheldelin, Andrea Kupfer Schneider, and Emily T. Amanatullah, "Women at the Bargaining Table: Pitfalls and Prospects." *Negotiation Journal*, April 2009. 10.1111/j.1571-9979.2009.00222.x

Ury, William. *Getting Past No: Negotiating in Difficult Situations*. New York: Bantam Books, 1993.

———, and Fisher, Roger. *Getting to Yes: Negotiating Agreement Without Giving In*. New York: Penguin Books, 1981.

Van Gennep, Arnold. *Rites of Passage*, 2nd ed. Chicago: University of Chicago, 2019.

Van Middendorp, Sergej. *Embodying Metaphors in Systems: Explorations in the Philosophy of Improvisation, Design, and Communication*. Delft: Eburon Academic Publishers, 2017.

Voss, Patrice, Maryse E.Thomas, J. Miguel Cisneros-Franco, and Etienne de Villers-Sidani, "Dynamic Brains and the Changing Rules of Neuroplasticity: Implications for Learning and Recovery." *Frontiers in Psychology*, 8 (October 2017): 1657. https://doi.org/10.3389/fpsyg.2017.01657

Wallace, Kelly. "After #MeToo, More Women Feeling Empowered." https://www.cnn.com/2017/12/27/health/sexual-harassment-women-empowerment/index.html

Zheltyakova, Maya, Maxim Kireev, Alexander Korotkov, and Svyatoslav Medvedev, "Neural Mechanisms of Deception in a Social Context: An fMRI Replication Study." *Scientific Reports*, 10:10713 (2020): 1–12.

Index

About the Author

Having been an educator for her entire adult life, Beth Fisher-Yoshida wrote this book out of her belief that people contribute to creating the situations in which they work and live and, therefore, have the possibility of changing their circumstances. Making changes that move one in a positive direction occurs through learning and practice. Fisher-Yoshida has formally worked in the area of negotiation for about 30 years, and the focus of some of that research and practice has been with women. Some of the lessons gleaned over the years appear in this book.

Fisher-Yoshida grew up in the Bronx and graduated from the High School of Music & Art, studying art. As an undergraduate, she had a double major of Special Education and Art and earned two master's degrees, one in Special Education and the second in Organizational Development, which she earned after switching careers. Her PhD is in Human and Organizational Systems.

For a period of 13 years, Fisher-Yoshida lived in Japan, working as a resource teacher in an international school and then as a training manager at McKinsey & Company. She also studied art in Japan. She has been at Columbia University since the late 1990s, during which time she has published articles in peer-reviewed journals, co-authored and edited books, and contributed chapters to edited volumes.

Fisher-Yoshida loves to read, paint, spend time with family, and exercise; she traveled extensively before COVID and hopes to travel again.

Bold Story Press is a curated, woman-owned hybrid publishing company with a mission of publishing well-written stories by women. If your book is chosen for publication, our team of expert editors and designers will work with you to publish a professionally edited and designed book. Every woman has a story to tell. If you have written yours and want to explore publishing with Bold Story Press, contact us at https://boldstorypress.com.

BOLD
STORY
PRESS

The Bold Story Press logo, designed by Grace Arsenault, was inspired by the nom de plume, or pen name, a sad necessity at one time for female authors who wanted to publish. The woman's face hidden in the quill is the profile of Virginia Woolf, who, in addition to being an early feminist writer, founded and ran her own publishing company, Hogarth Press.

Made in the USA
Columbia, SC
26 September 2024

43158052R00167